The Misanthropist's Secret Love-Life

James Murphy

The Misanthropist's Secret Love-Life

© 2020 by James Murphy.

Published by
The Heretic's Press
London
www.hereticspress.co.uk

By the same author

The Art of Exile (poetry)
Lyrical Cynicism (poetry)
To Hell in a Handcart (playscript)
The Poets (playscript)
Disposophobia (playscript)
Handbook for the Damned (cultural & literary criticism)
Crash the Bus (novel)

ISBN 978-0-9567920-0-6
Kindle ISBN 978-0-9567920-1-3

© 2020
The Heretic's Press
www.hereticspress.co.uk

Cover design by Chris Derrick www.unauthorizedmedia.com

For Joanna

The door that opens on the sunlit stair
Leads up and so the fated lover goes:
Loneliness is an abyss; love, a dare;
A steep ascent the challenge it bestows.

Even when death separates, love retreats
Only to retrace another time and place
Where patient fate can plot the maze of streets
That brings beloved strangers face-to-face

Born in 1957, James Murphy grew up in the suburbs of South London. He graduated in Philosophy from the University of East Anglia at Norwich. He then worked in several different fields (sometimes literally), including journalism and teaching. During the 1980s, he lived in Tuscany. He currently lives in Sussex. He has written two further collections of poetry, a novel, Crash the Bus, & three plays, *To Hell in a Handcart,* *The* *Poets* and *Disposophobia, as well as a cultural and literary critique, Handbook for the Damned.* He is married with a son.

Prologue

THE RULES OF ROMANTICISM

An Icarian flight to the sun
The fast-burn of brief inspiration;
A fugitive freedom never quite won;
A spent force of elation.

You thirsted for drunkenness
No wine could assuage:
Only the lees of loneliness
Spilled on your page.

So fold up the foreign map,
Close your tired eyes,
Rest your head on my lap,
Lose track of the skies

To find a way, lose the way.
Give up all trace of a trail,
Forget the date and the day:
Memory is never to scale.

As borderless as loss,
As deep as childhood:
The dark paths you cross
Disappear in this wood

Where fact unravels
And certainty recedes;
Where the freed mind travels,
Dreaming whatever it needs.

At the borders of daylight,
And the margins of sleep,
Trust only in sunrise and twilight,
Things you can't keep.

CONTENTS

Part 4 – DOCTORED REPORTS

Part 5 – WOLFMAN

Part 6 – BANGED UP

Part 7 – THE SEDUCTIONS OF MEMORY

Part 8 – ESCAPE ATTEMPT

The Misanthropist's Secret Love Life

INTRODUCTION
Origins of The Misanthropist's Secret Love Life.

We labour under the loveless dispensation of a mechanistic age regulated by cheap, ideological platitudes, but, deep down, despite all our protestations, could it be that we secretly know we deserve it? Are we, in fact, unconsciously acute judges meting out to ourselves a condign punishment for the crime of mass-produced, spiritual indifference?

Certainly, it is a philosophical commonplace that with all the evidence of 20th century human cruelty before us, the holocausts and hecatombs, we in the west have suffered a tremendous blow to our capacity for faith - not just in religion and culture but in human nature itself; thus, in the jaundiced light of our proven capacity for duplicity and depravity, is it not logical implicitly to distrust, if not expressly to loathe the sight of, one's fellow human beings?

And yet, even in handing down this severest judgement on our own turpitude, perhaps some mitigating perspective is called for; perhaps, even in our cruelties, our age is not unique. Hasn't man always been capable of breath-taking wickedness? Weren't infants thrown from the ramparts of a broken-hearted Troy by the victorious Greeks? Should we, then, merely acknowledge the fact that our talent for cruelty has simply grown more technologically efficient; that, though we can destroy millions at the press of a button rather than waste time by firing off an arrow from a bow, nevertheless the quotient of our cruelty, our will to destroy, in both cases remains unchanged?

When beauty's deceptive, momentary blossom has fallen, universal misanthropy runs through our hearts like rings in a tree: the older the man the more rings there are. It begins with cynicism, which, nowadays, we learn almost at our mother's breast (assuming, somewhat optimistically, that we were breast-fed by today's militant feminist mother!). At the outset, cynicism may rightly be perceived as a weapon, a means of psychological self-defence against the daily onslaught mounted on our sensibility by a corrupt world of commercial interests and political falsehoods and their oleaginous proponents. Who can we trust? Certainly not the smug faces smiling from the TV, cocooned in their inane celebrity happiness; and maybe not our lover who ultimately has his or her own interests to protect; not even, in the final analysis, the protective institution of our own family which, in this time of social storm and stress, suffers its own distortions and wreaks its own internal vengeance on us as individuals. Then who? Ourselves alone? But surely we are the least trustworthy, since we know our vices only too well! Truly we are perfect cynics: so much so that we have learned to view even our own cynicism with distrust: indeed, is cynicism not merely evidence of the victim proverbially 'getting his retaliation in first' before life lets him down?

But when the cynic grows cynical even about his own cynicism, what is left? How, then, are we to live, to love - alone; how take the first step forward, into what kind of emotional landscape?

In this context, the firestorms of Hiroshima, Nagasaki and Dresden are compelling icons for modern imagination. For reasons we can rationalise historically until kingdom come, we have reduced ourselves and our cultures to actual as well as metaphorical rubble. The aesthetic and religious structures of Western tradition have been razed to the ground and, though technologically advanced, our identity is pixelated by the fine dust of a century of shattered illusions. The present is by now a well-known wasteland. Yet from somewhere within the eerie atmosphere of our alienated cityscapes the faint tones of strange music are still discerned, percolating as if via some unseen, malfunctioning PA system. What kind if music it is we can't quite make out, whether modern or medieval, secular or religious; but being addicted by nature to music - for all truths seduce us with melodies suited to our particular temperaments - we follow the sound to see where it comes from .

In this sense, *The Misanthropist's Secret Love Life* represents the individual's quest to find meaning amongst the post-modernist rubble of demotic triviality, rootless relativist values and cheap sensations. Hopefully, as such, *The Misanthropist* may serve as a guidebook accompanying the reader across a landscape the devastation of which is, whilst our gaze remains firmly blinkered, much starker than we choose to admit. And yet, though bleak at times, the journey undertaken through our modern underworld (accompanied in good faith by the Virgilian spirit of Imagination) ultimately leads back up towards the sunlight.

ii

Part psychological epic, part philosophical quest, *The Misanthropist* could also be said to constitute an arena in which so-called modern and classical aesthetic values come to grips with each other. Indeed, given that combatants can sometimes not only learn each other's strength and weaknesses but also acquire each other's skills, *The Misanthropist* embraces the collision between these opposing traditions.

In this context, in the Misanthropist's pages the moral influence of Theodor Adorno's stark dictum that 'there can be no art after Auschwitz' comes face to face with Beauty's eternal and equally ruthless force. For although (post)Modernism sought to get round Adorno's celebrated maxim by directly confronting - some would say, obsessing about - man's moral ugliness, insodoing the movement self-consciously took no account of Beauty's demands, which will not - cannot - be ignored by any artist embarked on a serious exploration of his vocation. Indeed, like the Old Testament deity, Beauty is a jealous god: mighty Aphrodite wreaks bitter revenge on any who do not pay her sufficient tribute. This she does simply by turning into Medusa, freezing them in their own moral, spiritual and aesthetic ugliness. Indeed, any attempt to deprive the human soul of access to, and experience of, beauty ultimately deforms it. By this measure we may construe the works of an artist such as Bacon as a sincere but grotesquely misguided and self-defeating celebration of deformity.

Other aesthetic dilemmas are also addressed in *The Misanthropist,* namely: the confrontation between our ultra urban-centric age and the eternal siren spirit of nature. City-life by definition, and however alienated, has a tendency to exalt collective values: what role, conversely, are solitude and silence to play in the modern pursuit of individuation in such a context? How is a balance to be struck in contemporary sensibility, beset at every step with the paramount allure of fame, celebrity and social success of all kinds? Again, in an age which prizes instant gratification on each and every level, how and to what extent is any individual to engage with the practise of discipline; how meaningfully embrace the principle of deferred gratification in the pursuit of a higher purpose ?

Wrestling with such questions *The Misanthropist* accepts that combat of any kind is rarely straightforward. When adversaries tangle, each masked by historical circumstance, we can lose sight of who is who and where our sympathies lie. In the fight for aesthetic truth, for example, should Realism or Imagination, Naturalism or Idealism win our allegiance? Should we shout for innovation or tradition? Then again, at what stage does innovation become the established tradition; moreover, does not innovation itself quickly become dogmatic and reactionary?

What is eternally certain is that ultimately we become what we concentrate our hearts and minds upon. Spiritually-speaking, and to put it crudely, we are what we eat. Materially rich in our age, we nevertheless live spiritually at subsistence level. Our 'culture' offers us a junk diet, a gallimaufry of savourless clichés and false epiphanies, a hotchpotch of half-baked revelations and badly-digested philosophy. *The Misanthropist* rejects this junk regime and embarks on its own asceticism in which everything that is not proved to nourish the spirit is rejected.

Of course, in adopting this radical viewpoint, *The Misanthropist* acknowledges that asceticism is itself a form of aesthetic extremism. As such - and as a book above all of poetic utterance - *The Misanthropist* necessarily deals in strong emotional stimulants. However, though its truths may at times taste bitter, it is to be hoped that they do so as tonics to a modern sensibility grown sluggish and enervated through too much comfortable psychological cliché. That said, *The Misanthropist* is concerned never to resort gratuitously to mere sensationalism in any of the moods and subjects it explores. Ultimately, the philosophical tenor of *The Misanthropist* remains very definitely one of hope - passionate faith, even - in human nature's ability to find a way out of its own, self-created existential alienation.

The question was posed earlier, 'when the cynic grows cynical even about his own cynicism, what is left?' Perhaps the answer is a door ajar, the pushing open of which will require a strange new confidence, itself leading onto the revelation of aspects of human nature long ago masked from view by our wilfully constricted materialist perspective. But all doors are ambiguous: there is no certainty as to what we will find on the other side of them. Indeed, as Alice discovered in Wonderland, the passageways or great rooms that doors give on to do not always lead to, or end up in, experiences that are pleasant, or whose significance is immediately apparent. Nevertheless, human curiosity is compulsive and doors are unavoidable: perhaps that's why we seek them out. Indeed, it could be said we have a congenital predisposition to the challenge that doors represent. Our first experience of life itself comes by virtue of a human portal back into the physical world: the door of our mother's body through which we pass, more or less kicking and screaming, is our first brush with the dynamic architecture and archetype of the gateways that serially confront us throughout life. Of course, as with individuals, so with cultures; and thus it is that in our post-industrial, post-religious, post-modern - even so-called 'post truth' age, we stand before a new door - and though it may temporarily appear otherwise, ultimately, there is probably no real choice other than to walk through and find out what's on the other side.

James Murphy

East Harting, Summer 2020

orn in the image of its patron deity, the spirit of poetry is beautiful, exuberant and sun-like, it bestows Apollonian clarity on the darkest interior landscape. However chaotic experience may prove, poetry always endows it with meaning and musical mood - the latter dictating the form a particular poem takes. In this regard poetry is protean - assuming whatever shape best suits its subject matter. This polymorphous capacity means that - contrary to the partisan claims made on its behalf over the 150 years - poetry is not to be identified exclusively with any particular form of expression; but rather includes them all within its infinite scope and purview.

Drinking, thus, from different wells under diverse skies, the poetry in *The Misanthropist's Secret Love-Life* draws its inspiration from various sources of the Western poetic tradition; As such, its varying moods may sing or speak in verse strict or free; may rhyme – or (pace the great William Blake) even make use of reason! – it may march to the drum or meditate according to the inner terrain it momentarily occupies.

Acknowledgements

As the narrative of the evolution of an artistic sensibility the MSLL goes back a long way – decades, both metaphorically and actually. Over the years a few generous friends have helped in its development and ultimate production; but however far back its origins can be traced, Joanna stands there waiting - not, of course, consciously for acknowledgement, but because I am always trying to catch up with my debt to her.

In problems of poetics and aesthetics, her critical insight cuts ruthlessly to the philosophical chase. No doubt due in part to her genius as a director, she has an unerring - and unnerving - eye for the precise detail which pinpoints the universal in the personal. Add to this her rare capacity for a kind of ruthless, yet empathic objectivity, and her influence has been comprehensive. But, of course, such is the spiritual fusion of friends within the crucible of life-long friendship that the destinies of those party to its mysterious process are inevitably married; be it metaphorically or, additionally, as in our case, actually. Long may the mystery continue profoundly to amaze, amuse and bemuse us both!

In the intense world of small independent publishers, no book comes together without a guiding light and a strong hand at the tiller of its physical production. For his creative urgency, professionalism, design skills and good-natured badgering; for his selfless help, his much-valued laughter and seriousness on the road to the MSLL's completion, I offer Marcus Fellowes the poor return of my deep gratitude.

Warmest thanks are also due to Jack Murphy who worked with dogged digital determination to improve the original design, pixelated quality, clarity and all-round composition of the unique image of the crow on the coffee sign that forms the centrepiece of the MSSL's front page. Chris Derrick of Unauthorizedmedia' then used his brilliant design skills to develop this further and turn in the beautiful front and back covers.

James Murphy East Harting, Summer 2020

C ontempt is a seductive emotion: it whispers in the ear of the disillusioned Romantic. Whenever ideals of friendship, love or ambition fail the test of experience, contempt utters acerbic words of consolation that leave an ironically sweet taste in the mouth, restoring the conscience grown liverish with self-doubt. Above all, narcotic in its immediacy, contempt fortifies the mind with bitterness, thus revitalising the life-blood that flows in the *Misanthropist's* veins, and thereby supplying the dynamic for revenge. Thereafter, wherever and whenever the misanthropist perceives a source of grievance or offence, contempt provides vital retaliatory power; indeed, by its very discharge, the misanthropist distances himself from his enemies and, seeing them as smaller, reassures himself of his own grandeur.

However, as an instrument of inverse self-esteem, contempt holds specific dangers for its user. In raising him up in his own mind, contempt leaves the misanthropist stranded on deceptively ambiguous high ground. The height gained becomes a fatal no-man's-land wherein the misanthropist surrenders himself up to vicious loneliness, and an abject and potentially pathological sense of alienation. Contempt no longer protects or consoles him. He must either locate some mysterious source of redemptive sympathy within himself or be destroyed by bitter isolation.

The ensuing search, at least as conducted in *The Misanthropist's Secret Love Life*, leads the unholy pilgrim through a landscape of aesthetic, emotional and philosophical ideals - whether desolated and vandalised, or still highly regulated, he pays due respect at all their shrines. In consulting their oracular power he questions the existential relevance to modernist sensibility of old and new concepts of beauty, ecstasy, love, alienation, noble versus actual poverty, the individual's relationship to nature, and ultimately his own experience of insanity and redemption. To the extent that the MSLL tells the story of an unfolding crisis and resolution, its poems are better read in sequence.

The Misanthropist's Secret
Love Life

Prelude

*"Will all drivers and passengers please return
to their cars,
as we are about to dock...'*

DUOLOGUE WITH A PUBLIC ADDRESS SYSTEM

Characters:
a loudspeaker,
a traveller

Sc. The port of Dover, England.

Ls - 'Quick ropes bind the ferry to the quay; clouds arrest a British sun:
Are you so eager to return to custody?'

Tr - *Judicious northern skies that limit our horizons!*

Ls - 'And your late love of Latin luxury, the freedom of the south?'

Tr - *The heat's a cage: abroad, I dreamt of the liberty of rain.*

Ls- 'Then why did you ever leave these temperate shores?'

Tr - *To escape a different kind of prison.*

Ls - 'In what gaol?'

Tr - *The claustrophobia of a comfortable routine,
The house-arrest of my convenient unhappiness.*

Ls - 'So why return? Why risk the jurisdiction of the past?'

Tr - *Because I'm tired of a fugitive's disguises,
Of life led on the run, albeit Mediterranean, in the sun.*

Ls - 'Then you'll be glad to hear an Atlantic depression is building up.'

Tr - *These stormy skies shall be my auspices:
My confession threatens 40 days of rain, a rising tide
To drown the rat-run of all my shameless memories.*

1

The return

MECHANICAL WHALE

Living abroad, one Latin night you wake and find
Your room engulfed by heat, and five years gone:
Expatriation has swallowed you whole,
But some memories prove indigestible:
It's time for Jonah to be disgorged again.

The ferry churns through soundless channel fog:
My whale is mechanical, its stomach full of cars -
Blowhole funnel belching diesel breath into the air.

Even now the vessel vomits me upon familiar shores.
But this time there'll be no biblical, prophetic book,
No contrition of kings or crowds, just an empty quay
And bored customs men who let you pass without a look.
Yard by yard my reckoning grows less distant,

And whether my leviathan proves wild or tame,
Its voyage sacred or profane, are tales I'll tell the instant
I remember who I am - and find out who to blame.

PROSTITUTE

Queues to get in or out of the seedy port: like a punter at a brothel, being British means mastering the business of coming and going, the commerce of 'coitus interruptus' with the Continent; means developing an intimate relationship with the mood of ports: one embraces their valedictory indifference as a matter of course. - A port is like a drab old prostitute who deals dispassionately with the intimacies of departures and arrivals. 'You've been away?' she curses as you pass through her., 'Life goes on!' - 'You're back..? One more punter to get through today. You're done? So get out of my way....'

One never leaves a port without a sense of shame: one somehow always exits by a shabby side-door, accessing decrepit daylight, full of regret at having had recourse to the guilty habit of coming home.

RENTED HOUSE

Your first fraught minutes are sacred with possibility:
We haven't yet desecrated you with designs
That will harden into concrete disappointments;

Haven't filled your perfectly un-appointed space
With tables, chairs and place-mats
And a set of friends and memories to match;

Haven't painted your walls buttermilk or meadowsweet
Or hung them with paintings of elsewhere;
Haven't curtained off the night, curtailed its violent beauty.

But we will. Already our plans trespass on your wilderness,
Leaving the footprint of our littleness.
Tomorrow we'll set traps to tame your monstrous emptiness,

And - transforming you into a safe home – destroy you.

IN BED

Hidden away, but not hard to detect,
Even in the soft moans of lovers,
Conscience is compelled to suspect
A complicity beneath the covers:

The unsuppressed voice, the sigh
In embrace in the depths of the night:
The anti-climactic, incipient cry -
The dawning despair of sexual delight.

NOTHING BUT BILLS

Since returning from abroad I've paid the bills,
Discharged old debts to friends and foes,
Registered with the utilities to reconnect my former life,
So why did no-one alert me to the lethal power of Spring,
Because, from the symbols on the package,
Spring is self-evidently charged with meaning.

So why wasn't I warned about Spring's capacity to shock,
The necessity to make careful connections
Between memory and hope, beauty and decay,
The need to handle the corresponding wires
Of my cortex with care - wires whose currents kill? Why
Is no manual enclosed with the potentially fatal power of Spring?

S pring may be many things, but it is not a natural event.

To the mind bent on careful accounting, Spring is a distraction, a knock at the door, an unsolicited package left on a mat. Even to pick it up is fatal.

Spring - this circular junk season whose flippant pages play their transient trick of beauty on the senses! I flick through its catalogue suns and skies; scan its glossy, air-brushed images of rebirth and renewal with shocking scepticism. What if I subscribe to its vogue for eternal youth and find it flawed as usual; find the year grows threadbare in autumn, leaving me with just another debt to disillusionment? Money doesn't grow on trees - but beauty does....

No, take its tragic blossom, its aphrodisiac perfumes and dump Spring in the bin in the hall. In life you may not get what you deserve, but you do get what you pay for: the return on the beliefs you subscribe to...

Ah but then again, free gifts are notoriously difficult to refuse, and in the hourly commerce of my hopes I hadn't reckoned on Nature's seductive liberality; hadn't bargained for the 0% interest, 'pay-nothing-'til-winter', morally bankrupt, conscience-corrupting beauty of Spring. It'd be a shame to waste it: at least give it a look; by-pass the bin, throw caution to the wind; - yes, bring my desires to book - take the catalogue in....

Bursting into petalled flame in the city square, the blossom tree burns like a heretic at the stake; its beauty is its blasphemy. For one brief week a year the traffic smog is perfumed and redeemed. Suddenly, in this hell of commuting, heaven is within reach.

Young lovers comingle in cafes like angels in a renaissance painting; a pedigree lapdog preens in a dowager's lap; queuing in pilgrimage to the shrines of checkout tills the religious fetishise with their mobile phones.

Outside their plate glass window the blossom tree burns on - a public auto-da-fe in the mouth of the rush hour. Shocked by the beauty of its confession, some passers by stop to watch but like any ghoulish show eventually the crowd grows tired. Pin-striped business potentates and fashionable dignitaries who've seen other Springs die for their ideals dozens of times before barely turn an eye. Eventually, even lovers' natural sympathy goes awry. And you and I, too, turn away as beauty's fuel burns out and petal-scented flakes of sacrificial ash fall like blossom from the sky.

W ay past midnight. Consummately, without effort, affectation or contrivance the city acquires the threat, suggestiveness and proportions of a bad dream.

Down alleyways, neon exits flash like jagged teeth. Drunken laughter breaches the darkness, exhaling Anglo-Saxon gutturals on breath rank with beer. Inside, a jaded demon's drum-beat pulses out the rhythm of cheap possession in metronomic anthems for the damned.

Out in the moonlit, blossom-scented street, searching out tonight's disciples, as yet unrecognised - Morpheus, the hallucinogenic god of dreams draws near, pausing briefly to provoke the apt response: 'who are you looking at, you fucking queer!'

W alking through the city late at night all kinds of animals are running on the loose: mating, ruminating, urinating, predators and prey: the feral, feline and ferret-eyed at play.

Picking my way back cautiously to the car, I come across a friendship freshly killed, the soul of a lover casually butchered in a bar, vultures picking over the bones of old disputes. Elsewhere, hunchbacked hyena-creatures laughing, heads thrown back; I feign indifference: in cities, curiosity is a virtue one learns to suppress – and besides, bipedal delight can sound so similar to distress.

Moreover, my zoology is weak: of the other animals, certain, seemingly more peaceable, upright apes confuse the most - so nearly human, yet still primitive, unresolved - their gestures clumsy, primate, unevolved. No doubt, under constant stress to gratify basic needs, to search and find, to mate and reproduce, they keep communication to a minimum. Unfortunately they see me as one of their own kind, and when they try to smile they, too, bare their teeth. Are they frightened, relieved or thrilled? Think quick: to be embraced by one entails a certain risk: am I about to be kissed - or killed?

My voting papers have arrived confirming my identity. Democracy! Fake Athenian relic! Empty sarcophagus! The body politic long-since rotted away, all that's left is the mummified rags of money! Must we, then, the lately ennobled, the dubiously enfranchised, shuffle like impotent, old-style communists past democracy's mummified corpse; form our five-yearly queue in doom-laden pilgrimage to the shady shrine of suffrage!

I take one final, fateful look at the names on offer in the voting booth and something in me turns first to stone. Is democracy no more than this? A 'poor, bare forked animal' with stunted choices on each hand? Do I merely drag my feet in a leprosarium for the disempowered?

With new-found illiteracy I spoil my paper, exit into the late afternoon May sunshine and squint at the Plane trees' dappled impressionistic art. Deemed by the respectable process of democracy a village idiot, let me then abstain from common sense, and vote for holy idleness! Elect none but the sun to do my dirty work!

But the sun clouds over as if to scorn my call for representation. A stealthy steward, he ministers to beauty alone. Her eminence grise, he appears everywhere and nowhere; and his sudden absence turns an earthly paradise into the overcast wilderness I inhabit. The sun's no intermediary. He knows his mistress, beauty, too well. Deaf to all solicitation, tyrannous Venus rules by decree. Those out of favour are condemned to the deadly oblivion of contentment in these faux Elysian suburbs filled with coffee table talk - the respectable postal districts of the heart which, like a spirit in the underworld, I now stalk.

Fastforwarding and freeze-framing the footage of the family reunion, I see a look of recognition flash in my sister's eyes: the camera has no conscience: it ought to, but, ruthlessly, never lies: there's no secret glance it won't treacherously digitise, and then present as photographic evidence of all our old, familiar lies.

Every other frame reveals a glimpse of the detachment my expression couldn't, or hadn't bothered to disguise: caught on camera without a licence for my beliefs, recorded with a forced smile that's out of date by years. 'I don't belong here', it betrayed – and so she did surmise; and thus those lacking frankness, in subtlety are wise…

Nor does the CCTV stop there: back home, my lover's caught me talking in my sleep: it seems my conscience has confessed to several criminal convictions about romance in the months since we returned. In company, friends, too, accuse me of smuggling back illicit quantities of regrets upon the ferry: cheap reminiscences lifted duty-free from European culture's hypermarket.

I owe it to them all to be more discreet, disown any hint of difference or distress: if I file my doubts with my passport in some draw, my heart may hide its sense of statelessness. But for how long remains to be seen - and suffered.

My species' social rituals are rigorous: births, deaths and marriages, parties for the terminally bored hold me in constant thrall, testing my allegiance between them or solitude: the invitation writing's on the wall: it's invidious to refuse selectively - integrity, consistency or cruelty, I'm not sure which, demands that I decline them all….

T he mantelpiece is a catwalk on which old photos parade unfashionable faces. Look at that shirt, that hair, that smile! The styles we wore in youth! The warp and weft of garish innocence and future guilt! No question, the looks seem tailored to the requirements of a neat, neurotic destiny.

But where did their patterns come from? Was I, then, sewn into the garments of my personality at birth by you, my seamstress-mother? Did father supply the material? Was my design a joint decision? What inspired the dubious brand that bears my name? What failed fashion house is ours? Why does our happiness look so dated? Who tutored you in this human couture?

Ah, but mother, I know too well you learned your craft at gloomy hands, had foisted on you by your own parents a dreary loveless leitmotif; yourself wore out the most threadbare cliché of all: the shapeless, all-enveloping sack-cloth of sexual guilt. And how inevitably, Oedipally uneasily those two words marry in the tragicomic fabric of one's Western mind! Sex: mother: mother: sex.

And, of course, the thread of connection winds unendingly back: your own mother had had her own story: an unmarried Edwardian pregnancy: a first child - your own sister - given away at birth. Sex thus confirmed its taboo iconic status in your mind: an inherited proof of original, familial sin and shame; while guilt, itself, became not just the means to an atonement, but a form of worship to a two-faced god of horrible ambiguity! A hydra-headed hag poisoning your own confidence and coming-of-age!

And then you once intimated – so obliquely I may be being melodramatic (you'd like that) – that you'd been raped; mentioned some sinister landlord's indecent proposal and subsequent use of force as a means of payment when your abandoned mother had fallen on hard times. So sex and money walk hand-in-hand in your memory's forbidding, Protestant land.

But that was all a biblical life time ago: the lights have long gone out on those memories, mother, and I won't turn them on again. No. Leave the mantelpiece in shade. The positioning of its celluloid mausoleum is correct: husband, brother, children: me next to my sister, both of us adjacent to your own mother. - Wiser to leave all darker connections unmade: you might see the photographs too clearly, without the tint of sepia that memory confers. Best let the camera lie, its false impressions framed, all deeper truth betrayed.

'Italy, eh? So what did you learn on your voyage of discovery?'
- *What the ancients said is true: the world is flat.*

'Yet you managed to avoid the edge!'
- *There they lied: there's no abyss deeper than the human heart.*

'Do I detect the hint of a confession?'
- *What else is conversation?*

'You make it sound like an interrogation.
- *Isn't every heart a gaol?*

'Only if you make it one!'
- *Conscience is a reluctant fugitive: no matter how far it roams*
  It returns to previous convictions.

'Then maybe you deserve the sentence imposed by your own
dissatisfaction with your fellow men?'
- *Even as we eat, my appeal is up*
  before the faithless jury of these well-fed faces.

'You'll find them somewhat prejudiced by Pouilly-Fuissé.'
- *Such was the court of peers I fled,*
  The failed conspiracy of the life I led.

'Come to mention it, you never did reveal your original crime?'
- *The one thing unforgivable: I lacked manners.*

'And for that you stand condemned to a life-sentence
of truffles and linguine?
- *A choice of execution at the hands of other people's etiquette,*
  Or suicide by a gorgeous display of dinner-table niceties.

'I take it you've always been disgusted by life's simple pleasures?'
- *On the contrary, I've gorged myself on pleasantries*
and diplomacy has ruined my digestion.

DINNER-PARTY POST-MORTEM INTIMACY

Wine quickened conversation dying on its feet: fundamentalism,
The gender wars, society versus solitude,
Polygamy or polyandry, the vanity of free love, communalism.

'Where does fidelity fit in your erotic, solipsistic universe',
She asked, acidly. - Gamely defending me,
You denied my ideal state was Onanistic or misogynous.

I weighed in along self-righteous lines "Surely 'relatedness',
Is what we want: a quality of being with each other,
A dynamic reciprocity charged with self-awareness;

Set against 'relationship': the romantic hearse-and-carriage,
The diversionary waste of time
That careers down into the dead-end of unhappy marriage..."

The drunken bombast of this eluded me, nor did it go down well
With more sober dispositions: husbands
Who hoped - or wives who knew – that I would burn in hell.

The night wore on, the wine and guests wore off unmissed:
We tackled the washing-up together,
Rued the money spent on getting third-rate spirits pissed.

Inviting people is no longer simple: it involves the dialectical:
Dates, babysitters, the impossible versus the available:
The mediocre synthesis of the desirable with the practical.

Is it me - or do complexities increase with age? I could make a list.
You sighed and set the alarm: long gone
The time when we could just have laughed them off - and kissed.

SIMPLE PLEASURES?

The sun on one's back; work with one's hands;
Wine in the evening; a hot bath with a book;
A languorous gesture, a laugh, a humorous look;

Standing on the edge of evening, diving into the flow
Of the high street, the shoal-shimmering shiver
Of crowds changing directions; idle chatter

On corners, old men and women locking horns;
Inconsequential philosophy in cafes, ice cream,
On hot days, a lightness of touch in discussions;

Couples in love beyond all bounds of reason,
Striking theatrical poses in timeless tableaux:
The naivety of romance in its short-lived season;

Back home, the intimacy of silence or laughter,
A fire in the hearth, the kitchen's aroma,
Food on the table, the sofa and drowsiness after -

All relieve the dyspepsia of rumbling, ulcerous despair;
But the appetite for abandonment returns: - always
This hunger for rapture, a ravening ecstasy beyond compare.

2

Dead Broke

I could build a house from all the books I've read:
Maybe that's why my thoughts smell musty -
All their attic authors are long dead.

If real wisdom wanders freely with no roof above its head,
Let me, too, a lucky beggar, sleep
With no fixed abode beneath the stars instead.

Until now I was always rich in rhetoric,
Relied on borrowed truths
To buy relief from my anxiety.

But now the overdraft's run out:
My mind is bankrupt of counterfeit beliefs,
And, strangely, the relief is palpable:

I'm at peace in certain mental dereliction:
No lie pays off the wind and rain,
Reality demands nothing of me but my soul.

Sometimes I sit and watch the person that was myself
Pass by and tip loose change into my hat,
But I don't want his charitable, junk-food for thought -

My future regimen is simple: a beggar, maybe,
But one with a stately taste for equanimity - henceforth
Let's live or starve to death on choicest scraps of certainty.

IGNOBLE POVERTY

Sadly, for those who would dine at her table,
Virtue's menu does not come cheap,
Nor is it pinned to every high street restaurant door;
And to cap it all old my old hunger pangs
Are sharper than I foresaw:

I retain a trashy appetite, an insatiable taste
For highly-sauced exotic dishes.
I'm no Zen monk: 'nothing' is *not* what I want;
For every ascetic thought I conjure forth,
My discontent dreams up a thousand wishes.

Retreating from the frontline of my desires, I withdraw into a succession of quiet rooms, and listen to the city's conflict rage outside my window.

But there's a danger in decamping to this safe distance: one drinks daily deeper of vapid introspection. Like an attic with no light switch, I search within myself and see nothing but dark space: my mind trips over ideas of no consequence. I lack all perspective. I progress uncertainly, as if blind, towards the source of any light. Or perhaps not blind, but dead? Maybe I haunt my own mind like a ghost imprisoned in a tomb.

What is any attic but a mausoleum wherein we lay to rest the mementoes we find it hard to part with; wherein we pay respect to what we almost want, but know we'll never need again?

Looked at in this jaundiced light memory, itself, is thus a repository of possessions we want to betray but can't; our last unsevered link with childhood: old school reports, boxes of books we grew out of; photographs of places we fell out of love with, clothes that went out of fashion suddenly, like the love affairs they went with: that orange dress, striped jacket, an old hat – whole wardrobes of foregone personalities! Stacked in the vault of the attic still awaiting our return! - That suit laid out lacks only a body to make it a living corpse.

And then the books! - Archived lives no longer in print. - The attic is a private doomsday library, a tomb of books that betray one's cultural heritage; the ignoble genealogy of superceded wisdom wherein rest one's thin bloodline and lack of worth: the family likenesses are unmistakable: here lie all the shameful ancestors of one's old desires. Look: you can trace the errors all the way back to your birth....

Ｈow fatally the view from any window palls! City square, secluded garden or sunlit sea: with habituation, their novelty wears off like a drug, and with it the hallucination life should be.

Is there, then, no escape from one's own banality, no aphrodisiac outside transient lust, romance or religiosity to leave one permanently in love with life? - I stand in need of some mind-altering extremity. And yet I have no nerve for hallucinogens. Humbled by vicious nightmares and a lurid capacity for self-disgust, my taste is more for intoxicants that intensify a sense of meaning rather than those that distort the shapes I see: the world is beautiful enough, its phantasmagoria need no rearrangement.

Yet consciousness needs an additive. *There must be a drug of choice.* Human nature is hard-wired for rapture: the rational mind kills all it contacts: transport and euphoria wither at its touch. The rational is a kind of cold turkey from which imagination recoils in pain.

Then again, try to dull the misery of withdrawal with psychotropic plants, speed up with cocaine, or ferment one's spirits in champagne, still their anaesthetic wears off just the same: you awake to a terrifying small room again, with a sense of being duped and cheated by last night's show, the third-rate tricks, the vaudeville that drugs play upon the mind: the slow-motion slapstick and farce, the bad jokes, fall-guys and girls, the sloppy, soppy forms of lust and love played out before the gullible audience of dulled judgement, dormant thought.

Of course, all beauty fades. But why? Beyond the transience of the rose, summer's love and laughter, youth that flares, and age that fades thereafter, there must be a beauty that survives the beautiful forms that die; there must be, surely, somewhere in this dark a door, a lock that waits to take an as yet uncut key....

Second to none for distractions, London is the trick of a grand illusionist! Today, having bought a ticket for his show, I followed the crowd to the venue, they seemed to know which way to go: but suddenly the very irony of crowds diverted me.

But threatened by their anonymity - my Narcissism searching anxiously for its echo - I was stopped in my tracks by my reflection in a Kings Road window; not, as it happens, by the imperious cut of my own gybe, but by the sudden, antiquated four-square sense of solitude afforded by the high street's sudden plate glass hall of mirrors. There is surely nothing less distorted, plain, inflexible; indeed, less modern, fashionable, and ultimately marketable - than solitude!

It was then that I realised my journey on the tube was unnecessary; that there was a short-cut I could take to the unmissable event just by looking in this mirror; that seats were un-numbered, admission automatic, the venue everywhere; that, when all was said and done, *I* was the gallery and show I'd come to visit: my arcane, prelapsarian loneliness its most prized and primitive exhibit....

SOLITUDE AS A MUSEUM-PIECE

Solitude - even the word has an antiquated sound, and seems to designate an obsolete indulgence deserving only of supercilious, urbane dinner-party comment. So, too, mentioned in the same Sauvignon-Blanc breath, related words, such as 'meditative, 'soul', 'rapture', 'divinity' and 'beauty' seem as porcelain and passé as Chinese vases on a shelf... Are there, then, a set of experiences whose style and ornamentation consign them to culture's anterooms in the museum of the modern mind? - Say, for example, the quaint, unfrequented exhibition of the contemplative life? Or might such words as 'sin, 'ascetic', 'gnosis' and 'epiphany', once in everyday use, like a pot or pan, old sword or battered shield, come once again to hand, as naturally as car keys or a mobile phone?

In London today: itself a museum of the mind, I find myself both fascinated and repelled by exhibitions: the forms of beauty fatally preserved, the dangerous truths too well-contained: the remote intangible stuff of glass cabinets and special interest, the domain of stuffed shirts immured in musty corduroy, serviced by epicene, repressed assistants and style-less secretaries whose attention to detail is second to none, but whose neglect of the single vital detail of their own happiness foretells their spinsterish downfall each dusk at museum closing time? Exiting the swing-doors is a relief, and yet the museum leaves a taint: its patina of desuetude brushes off on me: my capacity for real belief in their exhibits fades like a threadbare Napoleonic tapestry.

I've spent the recent past ruthlessly emptying my mind of its backlog of superceded categories, but, like so much else, I begin to doubt the validity of this pursuit of late: the purview of the contemplative life may be open to debate, but does, at least, imply that there must be something left within the mind to contemplate....

I long for the warmth of the crowd.
Solitude is a cold, benighted theatre
Where wit is not called upon
Nor wisdom applauded:
Solitude deafens with its silence.

I long for the crowd:
My virtues are all social,
'I' am a social construct
That collapses without support.
Why can I not bear the weight

Of my own aloneness? Why have I
No cornerstone of love for myself?
I long for the warmth of the crowd,
Solitude is a cold, benighted theatre:
- And yet I am drawn in….

Step this way for adult entertainment!
Neon streaks the haggard, urban dusk -
A latecomer at life's third-rate cabaret,
I find I've paid for a restricted view:

The house-wine is over-priced and sour,
The women past their best - nor are
Their siren songs believable: near or far,
Beauty palls when paid for by the hour.

Fuck the proles' and bourgeoisie's banal myopic gaze,
The TV peep-show, the camp, theatrical binocular!
Verandas shimmer on Himalaya, Alp and Pyrenees!
The less humanity, the more I find the view spectacular!

HORROR POEM

You shudder at the nightmare:
The sick embrace and withered touch,
The ghoul that feeds on foetid air,
The manacle, calliper and crutch,
The morbid guilt no heart can bear,
The twisted face of human horror,
The soul of love disfigured,
The gorgon gazing in the mirror,
The venom and the hatred triggered,
The looks that kill, the arms that hack,
The mental ancestry of terror,
The lunatics bound back to back,
The cruel entanglements of error,
The bloody chain of victims,
The barbed wire centuries, sadistic,
The millennia of broken limbs,
The sex-crimes, biblical or journalistic,
The murder of slum urchins,
The rape of Sabine virgins,
The rapine and tortures legitimised,
The concatenated genocides,
The helpless inmates sodomised,
The plague-struck peasantry and regicides,
The corridors of dark rooms,
The sobbing and untended aches,
The stench of living tombs,
The thumbscrew, wrack and fiery stakes:
The electric goad and cattle-prod,
The cries for mercy deaf and dumb,
The silence of a heedless god,
The forlorn hope and body numb,
The choir of screams
With which death accompanies
His macabre, unorchestrated dreams…
Yes, you shudder at all these –

And welcome dawn as it restores to mind a range
Of comfortable suburban miseries:
Rendezvous we can arrange
With our resentments as we please:
A list of pencilled-in appointments
With sullenness and umbrage;
Of self-fulfilling disappointments,
And depressing trips to Tunbridge;
The needless insult, or thought unkind,
The numerous serpentine offences
That spring to poisoned mind
And puncture thin-skinned defences –
Take the way you slighted me behind my back:
I could whimper and ignore it
Or set pride snarling on your track.
My petty manhunt means there's nothing for it:
Our body politic of friendship, never much alive,
Belly-up reveals cadaverous worms:
So why not let honest bad blood thrive:
No more the happy smile 'hallo' that squirms,
But the face of frank contempt instead.
To show you just who's boss,
I'll cut you and your self-satisfaction dead -
So sharp you'll barely feel the loss.
Your body will bear no bruise or slash,
Outwardly, you'll look just fine:
There'll be no clue or social sign of any clash:
But the secret pleasure will be mine,
Yes, I must have old-fashioned satisfaction,
Because you slighted me last night,
This duel of manners calls for epistolary action,
It's each man to his fencing station:
E-mails at dawn! Brutal but still, of course, polite
Our act of mutual bourgeois detestation:
Count on it: I'll shed your piss-poor blood without a fight.

No more ill-will! – Ill will:
The foul air of resentment farted,
The gut-ache of the poor in spirit,
The residue of the spastic-colon hearted,
The diarrhoea of thin demerit.

No. No more ill-will.
My motives for this renunciation
Are, as ever, viscerally selfish:
Ill will causes my spirit indigestion:
Is, menu-wise, my shellfish.

So no more ill-will:
Ill-will whose morbid swollen vein
Gestates gustatory nightmares,
Dumping surplus acid in the brain
From unprocessed rotting cares.

Give me, instead, a spiritual digestive,
An unobstructed peristalsis of goodwill
To convert all the shit sent down from above,
Enrich my blood, nourish it from swill -
Give me? - Yes! a heart transfused with love.

3

Love in purgatory

Looking back,
We might never have met,
But in those dry London days
Of teacherly salaries and arid hack work
There was arson afoot:
Our disaffection was tinder,
Our boredom a box:
Fate is inflammable.
Passing by on the stairs
Up to that rickety flat,
We might never have met
But this was the catch:
Your laughter was petrol
And I lit a match.

A PARADOX OF LOVE

Angelic or priapic, pure or lecherous,
Love is dependably treacherous:
Either devoted consorts die
Or boredom turns romantic love awry.
Whichever way,
At the end of a summer's day
Love's sunset is this:
Brief, the blood-red kiss
Before delight
Surrenders to a moonless winter's night.

IN BED ALONE AT NIGHT

Insomniac, alone in bed at night,
Sins of omission haunt me.
Defeated, abject, I offer no fight
As failed aspirations taunt me

With cankered guilt,
A broken will and weakening heart,
The blood of friendship spilt,
The conscience split apart.

GRAVE-ROBBER

The spirit of beauty has died in me.
She lies buried in an unmarked grave
In the cemetery of my memory.

I took her constancy for granted,
So her mystique vanished
And left me cold and unenchanted.

Now I take no vital pleasure
In anything I see, but live, instead,
By reason's sterile measure.

The city's noisy, neon catacombs
Deaden me; so, too, the cell
Where solitude rents out silent rooms.

If beauty's grave can be located,
Maybe it's in the depths
Where my remorse lies unconsecrated:

Maybe there I'll disinter her corpse,
Profane the graveyard
Where the grotesque raven gawps.

Endings are where I sense her most:
In sunset or stormy light,
I feel her presence like a ghost

That haunts the fatal yew trees,
As Spring rain and lilac perfume
Mix upon the evening breeze.

The grave and isolated moon above
Mock all philosophy:
We have no choice but to love.

Alone on the beach, looking out to sea,
I stand exposed to every agency of erosion;

Certainties that seemed so durable in youth
Are worn away by decades of wind and rain:

One's identity dissolves as deceptively as sandstone:
Invisibly, the cliffs change shape

And as the tidal light of day retreats
Dusk's undertow drags my thoughts into the past.

Like a child's sand castles levelled by the waves,
I lay their ruination firmly at your door:

Your love is my foundation, the door I enter in
The frame on which I've always leant;

Your absence, a sea that eats at their cement:
Such is the human blueprint,

The bare materials of our sea-defence:
We build the barrier knowing it can't last,

That it makes no sense.
Loneliness turns the heart to stone.

Why is it so petrifying to face the sea alone?
Why must we be constantly be shored up love?

ANOTHER KIND OF LOVE

Unless there exists a love without a tether;
That harnesses no heart
And binds no souls together;
Which, rather, loosened releases us
To fly impassioned and apart -
Co-pilots of wild Pegasus!

But enough of symbolic horses:
The history we know best
Teaches heartbreaks and divorces.
There never was a mythic beast
Imprisoned in the rib cage
Of the human breast
To love without attachment.
Leave dreamers to pagan theology:
Our myths are laws of physics:
Our ancestry, Darwinian biology:

Love's lore isn't traced in sacred books
But in the transport of hungry hearts,
Bodily desires and sultry looks,
Prosaic beds and primitive procreative parts:
My rhymeless, modern soul
Rejects love's courtly poetry,
Nor will an old romantic word order extol!

Subject to laws of time and gravity,
Modern love is worldly-wise;
Platonic love a cliché,
A dream of celestial skies,
A paradox of solitude,
A perversity of anchorites in deserts
Weird holy dudes with attitude;
The epiphany of monks in solitary cells;
The drink of mad ascetics,
Drawn from secret wells

Who thirst for the giving not the getting;
Who've found their answer
In detachment; in letting
Passion go; who love but want none in return,
And in loving that which appals
(The solitude we lesser lovers spurn),
Find redemption calls.

But their time is gone;
The great age of sacred books is past,
Its innocence antediluvian.
Ink and papyrus revelations cannot last,
Ancient truths bleach in the sun.
Divine love did not survive the flood,
Nor did the drowned saints of antisociability -

Or do we still carry a fever in our blood,
The DNA of being solitary?
Maybe we're fatally related,
Cousins, once-removed from the holy loneliness
Of the human family: cursed, belated,
Descendants of a congenital restlessness,
Doomed to be drawn to the saints' solution
To never feeling whole?
Doesn't solitude still whisper sedition
To the crowded modern soul?
Doesn't birth betray us into a singular tradition?

Isn't there a stillness in the heart?
Though we lose ourselves in multitudes
Don't we also long to find ourselves apart?
Aren't we and those antique holy fools
Both engaged in the same search
(though using different tools)
To craft a quietude that works;
A heart that functions without misery;
A love to mend distress,
A peace of mind that history
Ingenuously called holiness?

The simple paradox, it seems, is this:
In order to be offered, love must pre-exist
Desire - and outlast a kiss;
Must already echo in the chamber
Of the human breast.
Doesn't each soul contain a song,
The heart lay down a beat within each chest?
Doesn't Orpheus clamber
Down into hell's underworld
To sing life-giving tones
To Eurydice (laid like a dead leaf furled)
On a lyre he already owns?

Translated into modern myth:
Doesn't the poet pick up his pen
And draw breath
Responding to an echo heard within?
Isn't the artist in love with life,
Rapt in a reciprocity
That heals internal strife?
Why does polarity
Exist within the human heart,
Unless it creates a desire for unity
To make sense of life even as it falls apart?

More and more I begin to think,
Having been so long unobservant
Of all the clues left in blood, paint and ink,
That love's no servant
Waiting on desire's command;
That there's something
About love that I don't understand -
And that this 'something'
May, when all is said and done,
Be the illuminated manuscript of everything
Bleached to white under a blinding modern sun.

4

Doctored Reports

Leaves rot, the black rooks brood;
A dark romance lies hidden in this mood:

The year has fallen from grace;
Late autumn's putrescence gathers pace:

Bruised, unpicked apples pockmark the lawn,
Birds shiver in the rain, forlorn.

The day is dead. Nature itself lies terminal,
Pulseless, with no seed germinal.

Time itself lies moribund,
In a world the sun long ago abandoned.

'Winter' is a clinical euphemism for the year's last breath,
And as the epiglottal rattle in life's throat dies,

The Poet falsifies December's time and cause of death,
Doctors his report with dreams of rebirth, Spring and other lies.

SKELETON HEART

Trees denuded of leaves, branches bare as ribs,
Winter's skeletal landscape stands revealed:

Brittle-boned sunlight raps my windowpane:
Unwelcome relation to whom I feign absence:

I'm in no mood for his gallows humour -
My conscience already wears a noose,

And the body of my disillusionment hangs gibbetted,
A warning to miscreant ambitions on the loose.

Calcified, my heart rattles in its cage of bones:
My dreams haunt memories full of headstones.

S o: winter again. Winter, with its professional interest in - one might almost say, morbid proclivity for - housing the remains of dead things; winter, whose clinical cold emptiness compels an inquiry into the nature of what has died within us; - winter, that makes pathologists of us all.

Memory is our laboratory; regret, a scalpel: objectivity is all. Nothing survives of the past apart from our dissection of it, the pathologist's report into the cause of death: the aetiology of relationships, our analysis of guilt and blame: which resentments could've been prevented, which confidences rewarded - objectivity is all! - Or maybe not. Maybe objectivity itself is pathological?

I date and label my thoughts about our recent discord like clues; forensically anatomise the loss without locating it, until analysis becomes detached and itself almost academic; the act of reflection impersonal and sterile, a casual washing of hands, efficient and professional.

Ironically, one seeks distance for a closer understanding; seeks intimacy, but finds oneself removed, handing over to the Victorian attitude in black: the mortician that lays regrets cosmetically to rest, yet, unrelated, feels no grief himself.

In this mood I mourn no-one and nothing, am removed from my own life, leave no descendant hopes: - no contact address for son or wife.

5

Wolfman

De-civilised by doubt, I roam the streets,
Sift the refuse of throwaway remarks,
Batten on the remains
Of any petty kindnesses I find.

For warmth, I queue in supermarkets,
But a certain wildness plays about my eyes
And, suspicious of my dog-like friendliness,
The check-out girl avoids my gaze.

I forgot to shave this week. Indeed,
It may be that I am, in fact, a wolfman,
A creature smitten with the rabies of solitude,
Feverish with its forbidden truths.

As such, I carry an ironic contagion into the city:
An indiscriminate appetite for contact,
A careless, canine love of my own kind - I'll infect
Anyone with a weakness for laughter. Conversely,

Cursed with an uncanny nose for false refinement,
I bare my teeth at any threat of domestication,
Bite the hand that feeds me with tinned truths;
Prefer star-filled skies to a neat, suburban kennel.

For this the dog-catchers are on to me:
Marshallers of opinion, lovers of uniform,
Young and old, denim and pinstripe, cast
The net of sanctimony at my untamed thoughts.

And with good reason: one bite from me
Means an agonising transformation into a creature
That barks at the moon and howls for its mate;
Whose ferocious joys no love can satisfy or lust abate.

I changed shape once too often; burst out of my jacket and shirt at one dinner party too many; canines flashing, eyeballs bulging with wild opinions - compelled by my mad blood to proposition unwitting strangers with beastly truths. Deftly, the silence of my dinner party host cast a net and, once ejected, the invitations stopped. Who could blame them, these good burghers of town life, fenced in by their own tameness, their love of little streets and flower pots and fear of the dark and distant hills?

At least they and I have both learned a vital lesson: honesty has teeth: it bites - and people do not like to be bitten.... Must intimacy then be confined to strangers in a bed? But no doubt my clumsy practise gave offence. And anyway, safely impounded now in 'solitary', who needs powers of communication?

Day, the kennel in which I pace, unveils its dismal corridor of light, the sun crackles like a faulty bulb. Turned back into a human I score my walls, measuring four square seasons, with primitive drawings of men and beasts and self-portraits of chimera containing both - though even I am forced to question whether there will be an audience for this art! In the meantime I prowl the confines of my thoughts: I liked eating people and wonder how long my food and I will be kept apart.

6

Banged up

How quickly the heart turns to cannibalism!

This gruel of solitude is thin, unpalatable. Force-fed daily on the same old thoughts, my sentiments consume themselves. My digestion is getting worse and yet I'm greedy for news of the outside world! Idle speculation supplies a morsel of hope: I gobble any gossip purveyed by the newspaper dieticians of democracy. But everything I read just makes me sick. Sometimes I think I'll give up eating altogether, but then I love my food and long for company. No, not for me the fate of the pleasure-denying anorexic. I'd rather swallow people whole, then bring them up. I'll plump for bingeing, be both the happy cannibal and hidden, hypocritical bulimic.

No sharp objects are allowed in solitary, lest inmates do damage to themselves. Ironically, memory's cracked mirror provides ample opportunity for self-harm! I've cut myself with vicious double-takes on more than occasion. Looking back: no wonder I ended up in here! That face and smile, those clothes, the company I kept all lead to this confined space which is my rightful place.

Being sentenced to wear the same face, the same uniform personality; being confined to the same, cramped soul for life, one could be forgiven for being driven to distraction. But, ironically - and embarrassingly - my conservative mind insists on keeping to the beaten track.

I shadow it at all the well-worn staging-posts: hope in Spring, passion in summer, regret in autumn, reflection in winter - the usual kind of thing. Secretly, I wish my mind would lose itself, subject itself to danger, satisfy my appetite for adventure. No doubt this is vicarious and cowardly, but I've begun to bury myself in novels: I read of plans for peace on earth, eternal summer. In here it rains. For one bred on spontaneity, ironically, it seems I must wear hope's restrainer, memory's patient chains...

No luck with the appeal. Apparently, on referral, my punishment more than fits the crime: this windowless cell accurately reflects my outlook; indeed, it demarcates the floor-plan of my mental limitations to the inch. That's the size of it, they said. 'If you don't like what you see, look in the mirror...'

And in an unforgiving light it's hard to disagree: the pure-in-soul would seize this opportunity, use this cell for meditation, this time for self-examination. Likewise, genius would revel in such confinement, need no view, no sunlight other than its own. Indeed, borne up by old-fashioned imaginative flight, genius would shake off its prison shackles, all inward chains of indolence and despair: all ties of earthly things; and, though with body still bound tight, escape its cell, vanishing in thin air, even as it sings, into its own blinding light...

But that's genius.

B lack days and insomniac white nights are my chequerboard. Drawn daily from box-shaped isolation, I am both sleepless king and attendant pawn; and having no-one but myself for opposition, my game of moral chess is peerless.

I've learned to foresee my own mental train of thoughts a mile off, trace an intricate trail of motives to its source. As a protégée of solitude, I've manoeuvred my life into a corner brilliantly: every way I turn I'm thwarted by guilt, sex or violence - checked by bishop, queen or knight: whichever stratagem I choose, it's clear I'll end up in the shite.

But I'll copy what that fat, old drunkard did to me aged ten - upset the board just when I was winning - who could bear being beaten by a kid? Yes, I'll tip the balance of my temperament right over: let's see reason reconstruct its winning position then! - My drunken fate can think again before it breathes the beery word 'checkmate'.

Nobody likes a goody-goody. Like the unwanted attentions of a prison chaplain, wisdom calls on me casually when it's too late; when there's already incommutable distress to alleviate: for wisdom to bother to act, it seems idiocy must already excruciate.

From this I deduce wisdom has a cruel sense of humour, for which it's never been reproached: unless cruelty is itself a hidden agency of truth which wisdom masks from view; making wisdom deceitful, and morality at best a shadowy authority; at worst, sadistic and capricious.

A word to the wise: distrust all sombre, black-clothed wisdom: all orthodoxy is suspicious – the truth, defrocked, is vicious.

Contrary to current, so-called 'Liberal' thinking, competition is a social adhesive inside prison, a form of love, almost. I exchange a constant banter with my inmates, and, if I may say so, my score is on the credit side; but still the odd defeat tastes bitter. Even now, after so much practise, I am still wise after the event....

But is it not in the nature of thought to be late; to be an accomplice after the fact; to gather itself up unpunctually and drop the objects in its possession whilst hurrying after experience, which it never quite catches up with...?

Thought is thus a novice in a spiritual discipline the danger of whose ultimate destination its mentor, experience, has the trickery and kindness to prevent it from seeing until too late: imagination is a beautiful, predatory wilderness at the edge of a manicured garden: thought's job is to kill itself by opening the gate.

7

The Seductions of memory

L ike an old lag, my memory passes the days by playing tricks on me which I pretend to fall for every time. 'Do you remember when...?' he says. 'No, really?' I reply incredulously.

God knows, memory's got to have some form of entertainment: it's hard to deny him this small pleasure at one's own expense.

Not that memory's fooled! Though we don't say anything, you catch him in a quiet moment, it shows on his stricken face: after all, as prisons go, the past is pretty much impregnable. Memory knows he's never getting out of here....

The mind-set in 'solitary' is as basic as the luxury: memories are switches that turn on the only lights. But then, the system is centuries old and breaks down repeatedly: so you either can't turn on the light, or worse, switch it off. Memory then becomes a room you can't exit from.

Typically, I am now stuck in childhood: I swore I'd never visit it again without my rubber boots. Its dark room gets no sun, is filled with tears, with childhood repressions, with hours of solitary anxieties and guilty fears concerning instinct, longing, lust; an inherited compulsion to confess the uncommitted sin of every imaginary desire: you, mother, would enter this room – and not kiss it better. Here you come now, saying: 'If you can't pull yourself together, you'll have to go to a child psychologist, and you don't want that, do you..?' Did I not?

And here's father, glum at the end of the bed throwing no further light. Our two faces full of shadows. Here's the famous evening when, in exasperation he addressed me, mid more tears, in my room, like a battalion captain - (all boys are earnest infantrymen in their father's army) - 'Look, whatever it is you've done, or think you've done, we just don't care, OK?'

And so the trip switch clicks back on! – Bright day! O hackneyed dawn of happiness! Biblical in epiphany, childish in relief, I recall guilt lifted like a witch's curse. As father quit the room, he left the door wide open to my future. But not all of me went through in one go. A guilty spirit remained; remained and watched as a young ghost left the room in pursuit of the man he would ultimately become; a man unwittingly armed with, and possessed by, the weapon of a double-edged mind; self-spiting, directed against itself: wounding, eviscerating him with the power of self-hate. The rest, as they say, is history, and therefore (as they fail to add) the future too.

Of course, there's more to a man's make-up than a mother's love - or lack thereof. But equally, to exonerate you, mother, would be itself an act of cowardice, a belated childish fear of your ghostly retribution: the retraction of that same maternal love. No, like credit: condemnation where condemnation's due! And, mother, I must confess I never felt more free than when free of you. So free, in fact, that this autocratic prison unveils a new facility in me: an unsettling capacity for compassion: a robust variant of love bred by impassioned objectivity. Of course, I'm still trialling this emotion and need subjects to put it to the test to find out if it's true; though, typically, mother, your natural distrust of innovation in the field of love demands I experiment on anyone but you....

CRACKPOT

Another thought occurs to me... - but then again, why?
Why, sensorily deprived, do I *have* any thoughts?
What power for ideation regenerates and will not die?

What lawless spirit dances, what libidinous Pan cavorts;
Spilling from my crackpot-mind into Reason's
Regulation-issue prison dish, what mercurial liquid sports?

M an is pent, his energy demands egress.

The only two pursuits in solitary confinement both begin with the letter 'm': - the other is meditation: a violent punishment for those with unquiet minds.

The consequences of this sensory deprivation can be seen in the permanent exhibition to which my dreams now add their own nightly contribution: distorted daubs of angels fending off man-beasts, women torn away: children laughing, crying - graffiti of loss and absence!

And yet, like cave drawings, their linear simplicity displays an indisputable authenticity that is starkly beautiful: man shorn of every artifice and falsehood, unsocialised, incontinent, undutiful: reduced to basic elements of survival, love and hate.

And yet, ironically, bodily imprisoned, imagination is set free, unchained from all convictions, beyond all rational remit, deaf to calls of conscience. And though Reason calls out vainly to return it to the wrack, it's far too late. Indeed, the more seductive Reason's argument, the more steadfastly my imagination wanders off the beaten track, strays deep into a dream-world, determined never to come back....

A PROVISIONAL DESPAIR

But there's a basic hypocrisy here:
I lament as if alone, deaf to the voice that calls;
Yet your love is the premise on which
The logic of my experimental isolation stands or falls.

There's a basic hypocrisy here:
I rely on you for contact with the world outside,
You are living proof I tell the truth,
You boost my faith, you confirm the others lied.

There's a basic hypocrisy here:
Your harmony modulates this threnody,
Only in the context of your love
Do I allow myself the luxury of melancholy.

There's a basic hypocrisy here:
No one sings or composes deep in despair:
Agony must pass before pen hits paper,
I may be past all care, but still I know that you are there....

NO MENTION OF GOD

No mention of god.
No call in here for the old religious fraud,
Peddling his quackery of sin and compensation,
Procuring in the moral marketplace like a medieval bawd.

No, there's no-one here
That didn't loudly self-select;
Whose transgressions didn't book the room,
And stipulate conditions: this place is purgatory for the elect.

In here the wardens rightly ridicule
Those convicts who recant and get religion;
Those who repent their spiritually felonious convictions: -
If you can't do the profane time, don't do the atheistic crime....

NO DESIRE TO BEAUTIFULLY THINK

My cell (am I prisoner or monk?) contains neat paper, pen and ink:
I've got time to put things in perspective, in order
Of priority, be objective, but sadly no desire to beautifully think.

My heart is full of animus, my head of thoughts fruitless and unkind,
I had a feeling about this when I sat down:
My tidy desk predestined doom – orderliness foretells a sterile mind.

T here's no better medium for bitter misunderstandings: with its clipped tones and clandestine physiognomy, the telephone perfects the technology of enmity.

Besides which, mother simply refused to understand: - this wasn't the first time I'd 'let her down': years ago (as she now told me) father told her I 'wouldn't come to much'!

But for god's sake, why should I go to the funeral? I'd had no contact with the deceased and now indisputably distant aunt (our family never having constituted a clan, nor held each other in sufficient regard to merit so much as the price of a stamp on a gaudy annual postcard). No, I batted not an eye at the old bird's death. Added to which, I was otherwise engaged: a gaol of my own making, maybe, but the regime of artistic solitude was rigorous. Anyway, couldn't mother go on her own? Did she really still need her hand held?

This heavy-weight resentment rebounded, the maternal gloves came off: sentiments were suddenly bare-knuckled. I was - three decades on - reminded of wiped bottoms and breast-feeding; called to remember the indignity of birth, the utter dependency of childhood, the debt of love unpaid, unrepayable! Then, castrating all communication, she put the phone down on my impotence....

Sent thus to bed without my supper, I performed a creditable impersonation of manhood: did some DIY, menial tasks about the house; would, perhaps, have gone to vespers, or written a letter, with a sharpened quill, had this been the 1550s, which is presumably the mind-set that mother's motives move in.

What is it you want, you women? Isn't it enough that life's river flows from your source? Must you control its course forever? Don't all rivers end up in oceans? Mustn't a man dive into a mortal cold sea, and risk nearly drowning to rescue his masculinity? Can he only break free of your current in death? *Is death the one last great masculine act?*

It's no good: I'll have to call mother back.

MY ADVOCATE

Your smile violates all depression's rigid rules.
Like a visitor lead into my loveless day,
You smuggle in the gift of intimacy,
Bringing proof of the sunlight
That beats down beyond these mental bars.

With your ease and clarity, effortlessly
You raise my spirits – like an advocate,
Overturn the prosecution evidence,
Lift my wintery guilt,
Confirm my innocence;

With your constancy reassure me
That everything is being done
To secure my release;
Insist that I myself must maintain hope,
Not let my standards slip.

Is it so obvious? Sometimes I wonder
Why you took on this case of friendship,
Who it is you see sitting before you?
Yet before I can ask the question
You're already gone.

How many more times must you visit me here;
You who know my face, my case so well?
You, whom no prison humiliation can deter;
And truly I would be ashamed at my circumstance,
If only I knew who you were....

8

Escape attempt

ESCAPE ATTEMPT

Slip time's chains, this convict stature!
Why should the heart endure another Spring:
To see such liberty enjoyed by Nature,
Yet be subjected to wintery imprisonment within?

Slip time's chains! Let the fugitive heart follow
Unfettered desire; take flight
With the casting wind and wheeling swallow:
Fly like a thief in the night!

Loosen restraint! Shed all compunction!
Refuse the sour wine of repentance and sorrow;
To the devil with guilt, god and unction;
Drink deep of the moment - to hell with tomorrow!

But Spring's rapture left without me punctually,
Like a connection my mind missed
On the line from the flower to its symbolic power.

On the platform assorted hopes tumbled out of my heart
Like possessions from a fugitive's suitcase:
There won't be another Spring train for a year....

Now in this waiting-room mirror my reflection stares back
Like a poster of a wanted man:
The other commuters must see how guilty I am!

No point in running to another line – they're on every station.
I'll give myself up to the men in dark uniform:
To the cold forces of regret and self-recrimination.

9

Oubliette

For the dirty protest of smearing my walls with the faeces of self-pity, they've removed me to another lower cell: this time an oubliette. They needn't have bothered: what is there to forget, since I can't recall my own name or my crime? Anyway, despair's a youthful luxury: I won't escape yet: you're only young once: enjoy its romance while you've got the time.

So, banged up alone again, I look to the view from my window for inspiration; in effect, depend on nature's company as on a cat - not unlike, I confess, a spinster, witch or widow: conversation and dumb love I thus derive from said animal alone.

Of course, where nature is concerned, I might as well talk to a stone. Forced to accept my affection, whatever the weather, whatever her mood, nature rejects me daily, without exception; is, herself, mute, feline and contemptuous - throws me impassively back upon my own resources, or simply spits!

Such, then, is the mysterious, reciprocal coprophagy of romance: I nourish myself upon contempt, and thus nature responds in inverse proportion to a perfect lover: the more incontinently I woo, the more she shits.

GUARDIAN DEMONS

Dark, implacable winter days; days that break
Only to scourge the trees and flay the hills;

Days whose suns flare briefly in winter's dungeon light
Only to foreshadow the flickering return of dusk;

Days that deepen into nights of oceanic solitude,
Whose dreams conscience is afraid to fathom.

Like drowned men, my thoughts drift
With the current of loneliness; drift undead,

As if awaiting a reprieve, yet almost fearing more
The saving arm that might drag them from these depths:

By what prayers invoked, or spells possessed;
At whose behest? By what angels or demons blessed?

And should each starless night conceive a cold dawn,
The spring prove barren and desire still-born,

Who then will invoke the wind and rain's decease,
Or stay the sombre trees' deep restlessness?

Who will break the seal of winter's sepulchre
And exorcise its unregenerate confines?

Whose guttering flame will light the dark stair
And survey the cold catafalques laid there;

Whose heart miss no beat at the sight
Of his own face corpse-cold in the shade?

Whose steady hand will then disturb its sleep,
And comfort him, so long an inmate of the gloom;

Whose arm guide him through the shadows deep,
Recessed in grief's vaulted catacomb?

And who, upon the threshold of day, will turn
To hold aloft the censer of the sun

And sanctify the dank, sepulchral landscape
With summer's votive perfumes?

Then who, the door behind forever closed,
Will step into the brilliant shadeless noon,

And so, commending grief to winter's careful art,
Thus cause at last the silent mourners to depart?

INSANATORIUM

As governors of a house of correction,
Nightmares are liberal tormentors.
Like a remedial school for the soul,
Nightmares at least have a curriculum to run:
Their lessons have boundaries:
You come and go after sleep,
Nightmares, you can wake up from...

Darkest dreams come in broad daylight:
Dull noondays lit by dead sunlight,
A mind pursued by macabre doubts
Into dark corners of conscience,
Confronted by fears with nowhere to run,
Desperate to stop and give up,
But with no sleep to wake up from.

And the faces of ghouls that press in
Are all you: the aberrant masks you fear:
Guilt, concupiscence, sexual disgust,
All the medieval mental contraptions are here:
A pathological reductionist distortion:
Every motive insanely, mendaciously reduced to the level
Of lubricious intent, salacious contortion:

Predatory pederasty, sadism, bestial sin,
Compulsive, obsessional violation,
Darkness pouring out from within.
A mouth vomiting dead foliage, humiliation
Tongue-tying whatever you utter:
Reason deposed - imagination disgraced -
A mind rolling around in the gutter:
Mouth dry, lips cold, eyes dead, love denied, soul defaced.

I lie medievally beyond reach in a diseased wood whose decaying trees bleed sap: a sunless prey to whatever loves woods like this.

And yet I've stopped short of the worst; stopped shy of being absorbed by the trees. I check my legs and arms: they do not stick out like dead branches. I have not joined the corporeal forest of self-murderers.

Though its cold canopy shutters the sun, swaying branches allow an access of arrhythmical light, like far-off lanterns signalling a way out west. I begin to see the wood for the trees: the boundary where nature begins and the borders of imagination come to an end; begin to map out reason's pitfalls, false treasures and traps: I could still stray, stumble and fall; there is still a poisonous sleep into which I could lapse, were it not for these steps that seem to lead on in their own way.

And I begin to love the sight of my feet, these slow, dutiful feet that tread through the begrudging, covetous mud; my feet that have always done my dirty work for me without reward; that have now taken over the reins of leadership when their captain reason turned coward. Suddenly the sound of your voice seems to find me by chance. Like a possession by the spirit of conviction, a force greater than doubt choreographs my burdensome, dutiful, slow dance. Like a benign siren's song, my feet's dead-march follows the tune of your voice. I should stop, but, thankfully, have no say in the matter: at last someone or something has seen fit to strip my perfidious reason of all choice...

PURGATORY

One dream forecast the end of it:
Dawn broke dark, masochistic, cruel:
Wind whipped the world flat!
Trees broken back in the gale,

Nature's function in turmoil,
Tormenting itself to destruction.
I cried out: 'There's no point! -
Can't you see, there's no point!'

The words echoed when I woke with a start:
'Can't you see, there's no point?'
Self-perpetuating disgust, violent self-hate....
Of course, it took more than a dream.

But gradually misery, like a storm, blew itself out.
Is the mind then merely subject to a minor climatology,
A local time and place of reckoning,
Or do its patterns shift within a darker meteorology?

Storms gather unforeseen over the ocean,
Break, die out with purposeless destructive force,
As if they'd never been: in the tempestuous heart
The cyclonic drift of who we are must run its course.

INVERTED FAIRY-TALE

Sunrise: my window opens like a 3D pop-up fairy-tale,
Birdsong, dawn light breaking through a mythical fog:
Woken from depression's curse, I smile and then inhale -
An ugly, half-daft prince kissed by a pretty frog.

10

Transfer to an open prison

Sober behaviour has earned me daily release
To the open compound of the High Street:
Provided I don't stray from accepted opinions,
I have full licence to mingle with the crowds.

But it's no good: teetotal for so long,
I reel with the intoxicant of strangers!
The heady brew of the human pantomime!
The music hall of clowns and villains!

The pinstriped platitudes and pencil skirts,
The lewd make-up and pompous masks,
The corny plots and third-rate scripts,
The cartoon heroes with their mythic tasks:

All make me laugh, but, sadly, inappropriately.
Suddenly I see that I've misunderstood the deal:
Though played for laughs, the farce is not for real,
The billboards lie - this show's a bloody tragedy.

TRANSFER TO AN OPEN PRISON

Fenced in only by self-confessed limitations,
My mind is now a minimum-security prison.

I'm tagged with a conscience that lights up
To locate myself at any given moment of the day,

My feelings are thus constrained within a tight circumference,
Lest they err and lose their way.

Venturing into the town's corporation gardens,
I now enjoy a sanitised view of nature. Glimpses of violent beauty:

Say, forked lightning, dead fox or carrion crow,
I dismiss as unhappy exceptions proving the insane rule;

But, unfortunately, the voices I hear
Are not just in my head:

The other prisoners out on licence are the neat rows of flowers:
Their captive beauty calls out to me,

And with my kiss I confer the curse
Of a soul on each of them.

Each night I smuggle some back to my open prison,
Unchecked in my memory, where they wilt more slowly;

There, we - the flowers and me - suffer a collective fate
Whose details they are too innocent to know:

Condemned to life's stay of execution, all we can do is wait,
Like convicts counting minutes on death row.

HALFWAY HOUSE

It's my first real winter in this halfway house:
My razor grazes the contours of my face,
My beard is turning grey, my hair is sparse
I don't think I'll stay too long in this place,

In case it locks my mind in one unchanging season:
Winter is an unfurnished let with no adornment,
The sun an absentee landlord, his central heating
Broken, the power cut, no luxury or ornament.

The logical conclusion of winter is eviction.
How did I fall foul of this legalistic mess?
What summary small print did I miss?
Was I out of my senses? Or too much in them?

How did I leave my heart with no redress?

NUT-CASE

Like a lunatic on day-release,
I scan the faces of the sane for information;
Habituated to the hard drug of disillusionment,
I am neither stimulated by their scorn,
Nor tranquillised by their indifference.

Driven by forces beyond my control,
I surrender charge of my moods,
Am epileptic in my joys and sorrows.
Prone to public outbursts of song,
My path is littered with embarrassed victims.

I fall in and out of love with waitresses,
Embrace strangers like long-lost brothers.
In old men's laughter I hear my long-dead father,
In old ladies' vagueness the deafness of my mother.
We're more closely-related than they can ever know,

Bound by ties of failure to one common ancestry:
I've traced all branches of the family tree:
The vicious likeness is there for all to see:
We're all bastards in a shameless line
Of cowardice and abortive attempts at ecstasy!

A t large, on parole, sadly I present no threat to society, am meek and can be approached (and reproached) by members of the public with absolute impunity. The board of authorities advise me to plan my time wisely, I begin to pencil in a few dates: birthday, deathday, end-of-the-world-day.

But the wall-planner lies: on closer inspection, there's no wall behind it: yet in supplying it the board prove wise: the wall-planner's days and weeks and monthly maps are paper-thin exclusions of eternity, a direct view of which would crush me with its gravity, annul my size and scale, my picture-frame proportion, reduce to dust my genteel prison of curtain-neat security. By necessity, it appears I live in miniature, my wall-planner an act of self-defence against all-pervasive solitude whose sun would blind me with its clarity.

Fortunately, I have only to avert my gaze, fix my eyes on brief affairs of love or business: pencil in or out: commitments are interchangeable: my wall-planner is, like others, flexible, its ink is not indelible. And should some unforetold event occur, say, a major cancellation in the form of death or illness by trickster chance begat – ye, should the very sky fall in upon my diary constellation – I need no holy book to paper over any crack – lo and behold! My Celotape and wall-planner were made for that.

L ooking across the room at you now, across half a century, it would be easy to blame you for everything, mother - so I will. Ah but it's too late now for that undercover, insurgent irony with which I used to tease you from your stronghold of impregnable propriety.

You're old, mother, you've surrendered any pretence of strength of will. You offer no defence: time has neutralised your danger: there's no-one left to fight. Age has disarmed you of your most lethal weapon: your nuclear power not to love me, to lay wintery waste to the corny landscape of my young and yearning soul.

Now, daylong you stare deep into the TV with a curious smile on your face, like a child trying to hear a secret whispered, but not quite heard; or maybe you do hear it, but don't get the joke. You always did have to be cajoled into confessing to the dark sin of a sense of humour.

But mother, how diminished you are! So small! Reduced even from what you were: arthritis has deformed your hand into a claw: I sit watching you spill your food, suck tea through a straw: osteoporosis: I feel your soul shrink in the onomatopoeic diagnosis. Now it's obscene to think you once constituted such a redoubtable enemy: you, who are now so weak, defenceless, powerless to pick up a pen or turn off a light; to mount any rear-guard defence of the bastion of grievance you once held to the last man. - You, who dominated us with that self-same smallness, who wielded your capacity for vulnerability, depression and pain against us.

Of course, we fought back with various strategies. Occasionally guerrilla tactics got dirty, as they do in families. Would we had all fought in the open! But - tragically - outwardly, we waged a more or less genteel civil war (the definition of a family!). Of course, we all survived, even with internal injuries, no doubt some broken bones grew back stronger than before. Yet, doubtless, too (also true to cliché), love was the main casualty - and yet its sacrifice bore fruit. Lacking love, one either loses faith in life, or learns to love oneself.

Anyway, where you and I are concerned, mother, all that soul-searching is past. You're old now, approaching death, and I see you as a simple human being in distress, and try to alleviate your anguish. I *do* pity you, and not always at arm's length; although I still find it hard to touch you. Yes, your tears bring forth my tears, But I mop mine up quickly and, leaving you consoled by the polished smiles on TV faces, step out of your private winter into a summer's day. Inevitable, I suppose: since childhood I've always had a disproportionate love of sunlight.

CODICIL

When you died, mother,
In church we all said the right things,
Then stood sheepishly around your grave.
Buried you with eternity and wedding rings :
Some idiot with a camera suggested we wave,
But our silence, incredulous, saved us this
And all the other indiscretions
Of an age so manifestly oblivious
Of death's arcane traditions.
Besides, the undertaker, vicar, solicitor - various
Men in suits well versed in death's legalese,
For whom words are vicarious,
Had already covered all our funerary needs.

For at such times
Words are business-like and mercantile:
They cover up our crimes,
Faithful to our wishes and the age's style.
As such, words broker our best interests,
At best, invest in truth;
At worst, defraud the depth of our experience:
When love dies intestate
Its riches revert to words -
Both executors and beneficiaries of our estate.
Formalities legitimise the bourgeois violence,
Leaving us as codicils upon a page
As words defraud love's silence.

11

Nature lessons

NATURE LESSONS

Modestly bent on revelation, I've enrolled in Nature lessons -
A contemplative course revered for unveiling mysteries!

But one week in, the facade has slipped. Behind closed doors,
Nature's methodology, the elements, proves duplicitous at best:

Her picture-postcard views and beauty are skin deep,
The landscape paintings just for tourists and visitors.

In reality, Nature's a danger to her students.
As a tutor she suffers from a god-complex. In Physics,

She uses lightning bolts; in geography and geology,
Parts the waves and splits the earth beneath devotees' feet.

In fact, rumours abound of Nature's demonic double life,
Of a murderess in love with destruction and decay,

A killer with a taste for infanticide:
She'll drown a child as soon as christen it,

Flood whole villages in a storm of rage,
Spread starvation and contagion without a care.

Those who bore her, she simply ignores to death -
Some call this method of despatch 'old age'.

And yet, eternal seductress that she is, her ageing beauty fascinates:
At best, my lust is vulnerable; at worst, I'm virginally vague:

The crueller she is the more I value her petty kindnesses,
Show me a rose and I'll forgive her a plague.

Fatally, I think I'm one of Nature's favourites: see how she operates:
On TV I watch the praying mantis lose his head even as he copulates!

S ome days Nature says nothing to me.

To confront her I ran up the hill and hooped my arms around the waist of the solitary chestnut tree. – But my lover proved wooden. Cursing my taste in women, I turned and saw how small the house was: as if a doll had stepped out of its life.

I am a plaything, locked in a nursery as big as a landscape. I can never grow up, cradled by a mother in the dotage of eternal pregnancy.

Sometimes I wonder if Nature even knows my name: moody matrix of things material, soulless mute provider - dominatrix…

My father, on the other hand, died before his time; before he could teach me (presumptuously assuming he knew) the cunning required to break free of the mother in woman; to throw off nature's excessive attentions, to sense when an embrace is a stranglehold; to prosecute a life without resort to the breast, beyond any call and response to romance, or nurture or any female behest; to consider the prospect of homelessness, to discard the doll's house, to take the low road to loneliness, to father one's own sense of purpose:

That might be taking the general direction towards masculinity:
That might be learning to be a man…

TONIGHT'S SHOW IS CANCELLED

The main effect of solitary confinement
Is an habitual alienation from man, beast and flower.

To combat this, my new open prison grants us fieldtrips
To the country to restore our sense of proportion!

So, being Spring, I look around
For the great earth mother's daring circus:

Her great parade of copulation! Her fertile display!
But where *is* the spectacular, the show? Nature's 'in flagrante delicto?'

Where, then, the cicadas? The fatal writhing snakes?
The screaming swifts? The shameless noise that rapture makes?

Where is everything and everyone?
Why are there no lovers or lounge-lizards sunbathing?

Why no shameless, flagrant, sunflowers?
Why no sun?

And why are there no complaints, no protests
About the great English earth mother's lack of fun?

Is my coach tour just too late? Is there something I should know? –
The landscape's silence answers with a nymph-like echo – no....

CONTRARY TO RUMOURS,
PAN IS NOT THE ONE GOD WHO IS DEAD

Did we but scrutinise her, nature is pornographic:
Significant, then, that we British don't.

In this we are helped by Mother Nature herself
Who turns prudish in colder North European climes.

She conceals her lust beneath painterly landscapes,
Disguising thus her passion and love-crimes.

By way of direct contrast, I've conceived a Latin fondness
For frank old Pan whom mortals loved of old:

Pan! Of dubious parentage! Sly, full of fun, amorous
Of unsuspecting maidens, fond of every trick:

Where are you when we need you - master of chaos,
With your humour, horns and shameless upright prick!

ILLICIT AFFAIR

Cliché of clichés: I've fallen in love with my teacher!
What chance do I have when she poses nude for me so readily?

Every time I look at Nature she throws off her clothes
Her curves are heaven's hills, hell's dark gorges.

If I ask for a more formal approach,
She ravishes my reasonableness with ecstasy.

Nature has no time for dunces that depend on logic:
No time for dialectic. Despising biology and botany,

Her only methodology is intoxication:
She deals in colours, perfumes, touch and taste.

Only when her students are incapacitated,
Does nature begin to lecture.

Thus my sober notebook stares,
Nature's unstable ink fades even as I write.

I can't see straight,
Let alone make any permanent mark in black on white.

I reel with the scent
Of honeysuckle and white lilac, sweet red wine;

And so, in happy failure - successfully dead-drunk,
Nature declares her highest seat of learning mine.

If art copies nature, why can't I copy people? My portraiture
Is an aberration: the light in the eye, the depth of the soul:
Time and again I show no perspectival grasp of human nature.

My sitters: fellow convicts drawn from every street
Of prison life - turn out caricatured,
Pin men and women with digital hands, pronged feet.

Myopia, maybe: but the closer I look the less I see:
The souls of my subjects are skin-deep :
Just what it is people see in themselves defeats me.

Where they exhibit laughter, I portray nervous cares -
No doubt it's my brush that's unsteady:
I've lost all sense of proportion in human affairs.

But have I, then, become a novice overnight,
An amateur in life,
Or have my standards risen to an unforgiving height?

Try 'Still Life' they say: but my broccoli's as tall as trees,
Nor have my objects any stillness, any life -
The globe artichokes I drew today turned out as small as peas.

As for Abstraction: my palette just gets confused with colour,
My canvas, drenched with passion, is drained
Of any meaning. Au contraire! Definition is what I actually desire:

A universal frame of reference: it doesn't matter if it's smaller.
Maybe I'll try my hand at 'miniature',
An ironic skill that makes the artist (at least in his eyes) taller!

Yes, I think I'll indulge in some artistic claustrophilia:
A love of enclosed spaces!
Who needs life-size people when their scale induces nausea?

UNNATURAL CURIOSITY

No doubt, like any artist Nature has subjects she excels at:
Skies, for example, are her forte:
As a celestial colourist, her dawns and sunsets are unmatched:

But in landscapes she does, we must admit, have limitations;
Even, dare we say, a lack of imagination:
Her over-use of green has to be seen to be believed.

As an aspiring expressionist her monochrome of green
Is mean; if a symbolist, then what does her green mean?
If pointillist, why fleck only flowers with colour,

With so much green splashed in between?
Addicted to these fruitless interrogatives,
I try to prune back nature's tangled motives:

Grass, leaf, stem, tree - all green: you must admit:
If nature colours our reactions, why always green?
Maybe it's the neutral colour she spills carelessly

Because it's valueless, and need not be significantly seen?
Maybe that's why I never noticed it before, but now
It's all I see - the stuff is everywhere: hung around,

On trees, lain strewn upon the ground
In such copious quantities it's obscene:
Forget any other question but this: even if she's careless,

Why is nature's refuse, her excess of genius green?
And what does it mean for those who've looked so long
And fruitlessly? Why, until now, have I never seen green?

CENSORED PAINTINGS

Dead branches frame the carrion crow,
His violent, sleek beauty a fatalistic gloss
Upon the sunset's dying glow.

Bleeding sap, diseased, the tree
On which he broods, dies slowly,
A sacrifice to Nature's parasitic mystery.

Such are nature's unpainterly confessions,
Her unexhibited canvasses:
Censored self-portraits full of devious expressions.

They lie in the store-room of her museum:
Withdrawn works of artlessness
Displaced in favour of cosmetic Romanticism.

They show nothing lives except by predatory artifice.
Nature supplies no means:
We wring survival from her by hard-won discoveries,

Yet still fall prey to the crow,
The fate of the tree: mere transactions
In nature's unsentimental quid pro quo.

LIGHTNING CONDUCTOR

Blasted, burnt, lightning-struck, charred black,
Still the lifeless tree serves as a throne
From which the kingly crow reigns necrophiliac:

My soul is a conduit for lightning -

Only I lack the tree's serviceable sense of balance,
The raven's aristocracy,
The cruel talent for endurance implicit in his talons.

MODERN GREEN MAN

What have I eaten?
My thoughts have poisoned me.

No perception stays down:
I disgorge whatever I see:

Paradox pours like a vine
From my mouth.

My dreams are in turmoil:
I regurgitate visceral truths.

A tangled bouquet of feelings
Snags its thorns in me:

Unwilled, a barbed identity
Has taken root in me,

And from my decomposition
Is metamorphosing into me:

I am a modern Green Man, born
From violent dissolution;

Ruthlessly he propagates
His new form of me:

His green blood flares.
In slow-motion his flowers

Thaw my winter-world:
And yet nature has no heart:

So what drives his sap up
Through the stems of my veins?

What pulses the demonic beat
Of his predatory beauty in me?

12

Beauty, ecstasy

Song. Dance. Orgasm, hysteria, the symbolic rending of limbs,
The Dionysian tearing apart of all reasonable things! Ecstasy!

Why? As a natural escape from reason's captive state:
The lethargies of law and logic, the inert rules of a bourgeois fate.

But how to distinguish authentic rapture from the banal fake,
The connoisseur's Bordeaux, the roué's kiss, the glutton's cake?

Violent brevity! - Pleasure that fades too tangibly,
Dies suddenly. Don't the French call climax 'the little death'?

So! Exclude everything that's momentary or, worse crime,
Ushers in its opposite – the bitter sobriety after sweet wine.

Surely there *must* be a rapture that transcends time;
That transfuses us with an excess eternal and divine!

LET'S BE RATIONAL ABOUT THIS

This desire for release, for bliss, may be germane,
But let's be rational about this: let's be reasonable,
Let's not get mythologically, Dionysianly carried away,

Like, say, princess Europa on the back of Zeus' bull,
Across rough waves out into Shiraz-coloured seas,
Never to be seen again by family, friend or foe. No.

Let's subject our perceptions, the chaos of experience,
The turbulence of the passions to scrutiny.
Let's *not* give in to every impulse; let's, for a moment,

Distance ourselves from our drives, be objective,
Set ourselves at one vital remove from immediacy,
Hold the world at arm's length, point at the moon;

Let's draw a line in the sand, set a measurement,
A ratio between love, sex and power - let's say,
'This far and no further!' to the desire for dominion.

Let's philosophise a soul into being, let's invent morality
As a means of raising ourselves above the beasts -
Above the beast in us. – Let's be civil, let's defeat nature,

Transcend basic needs, let's follow a preconceived plan,
Let's build cities with hypocausts and aqueducts,
Let science and reason be the servants of leisure,

So that we can then do more of what we really want!
Song. Dance. Orgasm, hysteria, the symbolic rending of limbs,
The Dionysian tearing apart of all reasonable things....

S olitude. Desk. Chair: beneath their calm composure lies a tense expectancy; namely, that from one's own banality, one may isolate a thought or two of beauty.... Thus, like a lunatic prospector sieving backwaters, one pans one's own ideas for gold, tipping endless dust into morning's fluent stream...

But surely the very fact that man *can* pan for gold, can recognise it when he sees it, can respond with delight to the sight of the beautiful, means that man *is* in some sense beautiful *himself* – at least during the act of response.

You may object that, by the same logic, the fact that a man can recognise French means he can already speak it; or again, that the fact that a man can conceive a chair means that he *is* a chair; but beauty is not a skill or a thing; beauty is a quality of mind *objectified* in a thing, which then has the power to call forth an identical quality in those that behold it.

Like goodness, beauty has power to waken our interior spirits from sleep, and to pass on this power with its touch. The beholder of beauty is a communicant in a pagan mass of awakening.

But what, then, of the harmony of numbers, the elegance of scientific demonstration? Ah but these are such distant relations to Venus that she hardly recognises them! Such pale echoes of her central melody, a mute sign-language mediated for the spiritually hard-of-hearing - like those ponderous souls who go to a concert and 'listen' whilst proudly following the sheet music on their laps. - No, beauty is anything but rational. It is not a construct or skill. It cannot be learned like French or acquired like carpentry, or ciphered by mathematical number. Beauty is an ecstatic rape of rationale - ruthless, immediate, overpowering and willingly embraced.

Above all, Beauty has no utility: you cannot exploit it. Solitude? Desk? Chair? Beauty's throne stands eternally unoccupied there. - Beauty is the intense love of the chair's design without feeling the need to sit on it. Beauty is the lunatic prospector successful, stupidly happy in his backwater: always finding the gold. And always tipping it back.

F act: having come into a small inheritance I once invested in a heavy (1Kg) gold bar and buried it in the garden. It was worth twenty seven thousand pounds. I didn't trust the bank with it then, just as I don't trust the world with my sense of beauty now, which I have also buried for safekeeping for the time being - that time being when I can afford to expose it to full view and redeem its value in men's eyes. For now in these brute, collectivist days, I remain miserly with its exhibition: this sense of beauty, this thrill at life's largesse, this sense of its gold bounteousness. And so I have hidden it. But it is there - only sometimes I forget precisely where.

Occasionally, in private, I stumble upon it and get it out just to wonder at it. The very sight of it sustains me. Then I put it back, before the vicious world can grab it and put it on their grubby television and get polemical about it. Beauty is not for the masses: epiphany is private.

Beauty is best kept to oneself - and the one or two others who appreciate that kind of thing. It makes it all the more exciting when we get together, like children, or maybe terrorists, to share the secret of our treasure, enjoy a private view of its power. Like the severed head of Medusa, beauty lies before our gaze: still infinitely volatile, ready to split the atom of the mind, a force silently demanding to be harnessed. One day we childish disciples of terror will let it out: and when we do, everything ugly will be destroyed.

THE UROBOROS OF BEAUTY AND SELF-LOVE

Cut off from human contact (matchmaker that I am),
I pass the hours marrying and divorcing irreconcilable beliefs:

To my mind, then, as twins, or something darker,
Self-love and beauty *must* be incestuous:

Our deepest longings - for security, ecstasy -
Father our perceptions;

Our desire for freedom
Dictates the colour of beauty's eyes:

Why else would I abhor these gloomy walls,
Adore the prison window's deep blue skies?

No, Venus displays a family likeness
That betrays the nature of our love:

Mind-born, her loveliness
Is incestuous:

We *parent* the goddess: in art, form and face
She comes forth from our humanity,

Her depths, our time and space,
Her shell drifts in upon our sea.

But split our divinity apart,
Declare life and beauty separate

And a disastrous divorce
Separates beauty from love's source.

The goddess recoils from us:
Objectified, she turns cold and petrifies,

As reason's dead hand touches her
And prophesies

100

The disease from which our passion
For her ultimately dies.

So we lament what we deserve to lack,
Weep for the goddess to come back.

But why would a goddess re-marry our mortality,
Why couple with deformity,

Once lost, we have one last choice:
Not tears but a lover's voice

Must woo her; our own loveliness
Must seduce divinity.

And be mysteriously empowered
By its grace -

Like Danae descended on by Zeus,
With gold-dust showered.

Love *is the source* of beauty -
The first-born of love's family.

But we deny her perverse paternity,
The bloodline of our daughter-sister-spouse,

And so, hounded by furies for eternity,
Renew the tragedy of our ancient blood-stained house.

Fool.

Beauty *must* elude definition. Being all-consuming, any splinter into rationalisation, in the distancing, objectifying act of rationalisation, merely delineates the loss of beauty, defines and dates the moment you lose it.

And yet... - Maybe formal symmetry? Harmony, ideal proportion? Yes, but don't a weapon, an implement of torture also possess these?

A composite of mathematical perfection, then? 1 to $^1/_2(\sqrt{5} + 1)$... some 'golden mean' prescribed by numbers! Beauty laughs. Is chaotic sunlight on the sea not beautiful?

OK, then: Hogarth's 'line of beauty'! The sacred serpentine 'S'! The life that abounds within the body's graceful bend! – Yes! And didn't Burke talk brilliantly about beauty always containing some strange or subtle 'irregularity?' that kept it from the clutches of boredom and decay..?

But it is bricks and squares and right-angles that build temples. And doesn't irregularity only become visible by embracing regularity?

Ah, Aphrodite! Goddess, above all, of confusion - praise where praise is due! Plotinus, Pythagoras, Plato and Kant - great men all bow down in comical praise of you! All cast the net of words round the flux of your marine, foam-born beauty. You smile and then elude them - and us - with universal felicity and facility, revealing only philosophers' love letters' pathetic fatuity...

Maybe, beauty, we keep faith in you at last *because* you defeat us: our enduring love lies in being unrequited: the tension of desire is all. Is not the same true of poetry and prose? Is not the spirit of poetry born in the struggle to get free from prose, to escape its ugly grasp? And mustn't prose forever remain in hot pursuit? So the blacksmith Vulcan always reaches out in vain to chase his wife, the lovely Venus!

And so (to replicate Vulcan's lovelorn, mechanical pursuit with our own leaden prose), maybe beauty, not being subject to the laws of language, number or reason, cannot be *defined*, but only *characterised* as a peaceful experience of ecstatic flux, a fusion of forces, a harmony of opposites, an atomic split releasing energy and tranquillity, an orgasmic containment and release felt simultaneously... Yawn. So Vulcan hammers out his verbal chains.

But from what? Whence flows the molten gold of his and our desire?

And why does beauty even ask for her own release? What is this imprisoned force that demands its liberty? - From the lunacy of rational close-confinement, what rapture seeks to destroy this prison-cell called personality?

B
ut, anyway, why would you even *want* to define beauty, unless you had the sort of mind that thought that by defining it you had somehow mastered beauty and, as it were, achieved a stable access to it?

But isn't beauty by definition unruly, borne up a flighty, volatile Pegasus: equine in energy, Hippocrene in flood, unconfinable by reason? - Why seek a key when no corral can exist, no stable and no door, much less a lock?

Ah deep within you the old Enlightenment lie lives on! You still think to tame Nature's destructive force, to rationalise away her horrific, beautiful chaos; still think to climb on rungs of Reason, right up to heaven, little knowing that the ladder goes on forever, without getting any nearer its goal; that the ladder you are scurrying up is, in fact, teetering in thin air, tottering away from the wrong wall - that you never were ascending, but were silently surrounded by ladders falling everywhere....

Like a devotee plunging from religious ecstasy
And falling back on reason to explain his faith:

The moment you move to define beauty
You betray a fatal lack of belief in it.

Was there, then, I wonder, a specific time, an hour, or clock hands upon the minute of that hour when the world stopped being beautiful to me? Does one's sense of beauty have its own youth and passage of that youth? Does it endure the ravages of age? Was it a sudden or slow death? Did this crisis strike like an artistic heart attack to slowly freeze the passion in my veins? Or did it happen over the years, like an atrophy, a dystrophy of my aesthetic sense? If so, what stopped nourishing my soul?

When did I stop loving the world? Was it money? Did I just run out of money? Is that it? Could I no longer afford to find things beautiful; no longer buy the time for contemplation whose credit keeps the hungry creature in our breast at bay?

Yes, that's it. I allowed myself to be distracted by a very civil beast: its wolf was at my door: a man with a wolfish visage demanding payment. The same wolf that's howled historically before the doors of every poet, painter and musician; howling the same howls to which they block their ears in the hope that it will eventually lose interest in its prey and go away.

Money is the sound of a wolf howling at dusk. The poet hears him and, believing even wolves can be tamed and redeemed, mistakenly tries to turn those howls into a song. That is how, singing the lament of money, the poet himself becomes another kind of wolf - and turns himself out of the house of joy at dusk.

DELIRIUM TREMENS

Beauty? Love? Loneliness? What terrain should I traverse before I die?
With a child's incessant questioning,
As these mental landscapes pass I repeat the remorseless question: why?

Art? Morality? Religion? The more I study each detail and proposal,
The more their dim-lit outlines blur, like lucubrations of a man
With too much time on his hands and too little skill at his disposal;

Or a dunce, whose brain the aetiologies of loss and pain befuddle.
Experience is a causeless ache I cannot pacify: the word 'because'
Is the local drug in cheap supply - and I have hit the bottle.

When we behold any beautiful object,
We study the reflection of our own capacity to love.

Thus beauty reveals our hidden identity:
We stand revealed by, and before, the things we love…

But this cuts both ways: as a goddess,
Beauty's irony is sharp, nor lacking a sense of fun:

The executioner loves his sword,
The assassin loves his gun.

BEAUTY AS BITCH-GODDESS

Maybe, when all is said and done,
The worship of beauty

Is just one more delusion
I suffer impotently.

Yes, the cult of the goddess is lovely –
But at the price of sanity.

In the demands she makes on her disciples,
This is the deal:

Beauty flays the hide from all pretences,
Reduces you to the bare bones of what you feel.

She blinds the flatterer, scorches with Medusan stare,
Scorns all mediocrity, kills without a care.

Beauty is coy only to seduce;
Then, when she has won your adoration,

She will slander, libel and traduce
Any false desire for reputation. Only in the dispensation

Of ruthless self-interest, or to antagonise
Her rivals, does Beauty give unstintingly;

But present her with the insult of compromise,
Beauty is vicious - Beauty will destroy you unthinkingly.

Once seduced by the sunshine of her grace,
No other warmth can satisfy, no other love suffice;
You're in thrall to Beauty: slave to her divine caprice:
Subject to her cult of poverty, loneliness, disgrace.

B eauty is a rebellious daughter: the more we impose patrician law or logic, the more we lose her love. But though publicly she laughs, spurning our menaces, privately our fatal parental shortcomings cause her pain, because she knows the separation hurts us; this parting that was always inevitable from the first.

For hers is no act of petty, personal vindictiveness; rather it is that, as a necessarily rootless soul, she is compelled to live as the spirit moves her.

Of course, we remind her of everything we've done for her, threaten to cast her out, cut her off, disown her - deny all memory of her, forget her face. As she leaves, we call out, curse her departing form, expect her to collapse in the hallway in compliant floods of tears, not realising that Beauty has already thrown on her favourite coat, pocketed her mobile phone, some cash, and, smiling at her own Mona Lisa image in the mirror, disappeared forever.

A year in conception and design, a hardwire flaw short-circuits the rose
That flares up in orange flame and dies in days:

Must beauty burn so much fuel for so short a flight,
Its fierce light subside to leave so long a night?

In the project for eternal happiness what fatal disproportion shows -
The rose no sooner seen than razed in beauty's blaze?

STRETCHER-BEARER

Brought in only yesterday,
Colour drains from the rose
And indicts the cause for which it dies:
This vase is beauty's last resting-place,
This sunlit room a hospice;
This shelf the fatal bed
In which it will not convalesce.

No surgery can stanch the rose-red blood that bleeds
Through a bandage of blossom.
And yet the rose must take some blame:
Its loveliness drew the line of fire,
The long-range wound of my desire:
Long ago the rose's fate was sealed:
Beauty is a battlefield.

13

Expiation

SNOWSCAPE AT DUSK

I.

Why is it so hard to walk this frozen boundary
And admit sole ownership of the estate?
Surveying the valley engraved with ice at dusk,
One shivers at how winter's forces desolate:

There is no guarantee of survival here:
To lethal isolation I am no less a prey,
Than the hunted fox or fallow deer
That bolt and find themselves astray –

Here, where all measurements dissolve;
Where snowdrifts deafen with their silence,
Time hangs heavy and leaden skies devolve
An inhuman weight of insignificance.

This is not man's world.
Its sun, once set, has set for good,
Its loneliness is too intense.
Darkness and ice demand his absence.

In pursuit of warmth, the eye searches
For chimney smoke or lighted window,
But, finding none, draws cold consolation
From one's own footprints in the snow.

And what use are these? A hand's span?
A step? When they can only calculate
An overwhelming distance? No, a sense of failure
Like winter, is bred in the bone - innate.

It's not the view obscured, but the open prospect
That destroys: the icy sunset is beautiful, but kills,
And who knows if there's any limit to the darkness,
Or the depth to which the snow drifts on the hills?

THE POWER OF TRESPASS

II.

But if we're not bound for any destination,
Why the sign-posts, the desire for dislocation?
Why gaze at sunset, moonrise, distant hills?
Why trespass on dangerous hallucinations?
What is it that transfixes, terrifies and thrills

About the horizon and the landscape we visit?
Why - if we never can succeed to its vast estate,
Does it call upon our duty and ancestral care?
Why, if we never can assume our rightful place
Or tame the terror of so much solitude and space?

The mind is an abandoned mansion discovered
On a winter walk; crudely corrugated, boarded up:
The keep-out signs test bourgeois propriety;
But having broken in; you feel at home: hoarded up
In silence, your solitude revels in its own society.

But beyond dusk, only a wise fool would dare
The mansion's dispossessed, dark corridors
To claim the legacy of loneliness; only such an heir
Might repossess the wealth of rich imaginings
Hidden deep within the doleful silence there;

Might sit alone as night begins to fall,
Keeping watch in the great hall,
Rejoicing in the voices that begin to call,
The haunted shadows of the flames
That dance above the fire upon the wall....

THE POWER OF ENDURANCE

A time comes when there is nothing to do but endure; when ice is etched on the inside of the window, and the lilac locked in the bud; when meditation is fixed on the dead fire in the grate, and a strengthening of resolve is proved in a dogged willingness to wait.

A time comes when there is nothing to do but endure; when you cast a zodiacal gaze at kaleidoscope skies, and see only meaningless stars; when, in accepting your fate, you get on with the cutting of firewood and kindling, the clearing of ash from the grate.

A time comes when there is nothing to do but endure; when endurance is a sacred renunciation, a statement of faith in the moods you create; when, working in the garden, reconciled to your state, purple perfume seeps into your mind and the lilac is suddenly lovelier for being so late.

WOUND

Late April:
Sunlight cauterises the shot-grey skies;
In the lanes, the arterial flow of rain is stanched,
Grass redresses old abrasions of bare earth:
Mud coagulates, winter's wound is healed at last,
Dark days are over, all struggle and all fever past....

Through windows
Of broken cloud, sunlight streams upon the stricken land
And gently wakes it from its convalescent dream,
Trees stretch out mortified, stiff branches,
Flowers open their sleep-ridden eyes:
Any moment, like a ghost restored to life, Spring will rise

And gaze on those
Who kept a faithful vigil during winter's midnight months.
What faces will she see? What voices hear? What names recall?
Spirit invested with so many hopes! Restored to us at last!
With what memories will she disinter our own deep-buried happiness,
With what revelation dissolve the snowdrift of our wintery lives?

On this first Spring day,
I have wandered around naked in the sun daylong:
My every thought open to interpretation;
My every sentiment exposed to full view.

I suffer from the childish exhibitionism of the innocent:
On my face I bear the lover's naive sign of longing;
For this I suffer the indignity of being completely ignored.
But I do not waver in my nudity. Fortunately, I have no shame.

Could it be that, where a sense of time is concerned, one is predisposed from birth - prejudiced even - in favour of a certain tense?

I ask because I seem to have been born in the breech of my own life, walking forward but looking back. Hence, forever bringing up the rear, exposed and vulnerable to the past, ironically, I occupy the vanguard of memory, am a veteran and expert in the art of retreat from life. I feel an acute affinity with things that go by too quickly: a moment's love or laughter, a morning's quicksilver sunlight....

Accordingly, in this professorship of nostalgia I'm un-discovering the need for new technology at an alarming rate - accelerating as each year passes by. This irreversible force called memory: I'm compiling a definitive study of the gravitational pull of what it pulls and why.

As a pioneer of ways back into the past, ultimately, I hope to discover the pathology of regret and discontent - things that never were of any utility to me or anyone... and so, eventually develop the prototype of a mysterious contentment that might last.

TRAVELLING AT THE SPEED OF LIFE

If desire is an accelerant, a quickening of the blood,
An increase in the heart-rate caused
By our longing to possess, it would imply that patience

Takes your foot off the gas; is a slowing down
Of our perceptions to the speed of life;
Of ideas occurring silently within the sound barrier.

Certainly, with my pedal no longer 'to the metal',
I begin to enjoy travelling more than arriving;
Moods that only threaten to break: storm clouds

Bleaching to fair weather, or thunder dying away;
Maybe a crow preening feathers on a wall
In a broken down barn or some abandoned place,

Unloved but lovely; maybe the scene of an unstolen kiss,
A romance unchanced - ordanariness enhanced. If moments
Of deep insignificance have a mystery, maybe it's this?

THE LAKE REVISITED

I drive by this lake most days,
Following life's banal highway code,
My mind bent on its B-road ways;
But today I stop, a debt is owed:

Gazing across the water,
I sense my mind decelerate
To a standstill with the swan
Adrift upon time's surface -

No desire takes wing to fly.
Driven on by no contingency
No distractions break
Cover. Instead, like the swan upon the lake,

I sit and wait without expectancy:
Secure, sedate,
Reconciled to autumn,
Still as fate.

ETYMOLOGY OF THE WORD 'DISMAL'

I'm inverting Roman lore: for me there are two days each moon
That seem inexplicably benign:
Their humours submit to no analysis, follow no rhyme or tune.

There seems to be no limit by which my new fortune is bounded:
This morning I woke in a good mood:
Ominously, this presentiment of content proved well-founded:

I worked, relaxed, sang ingenuously, cooked, enjoyed my food,
Slept, in dreams was humorously hounded
By comic situations: I'm edgy: this change of luck is far too crude.

Maybe I'm just getting old, but I'm increasingly susceptible to shadows: their beauty and superiority to substantial form: the subtle charm that haunts the dance of grasses ghosted on the sunlit wall....

So, too, for me the flickering calligraphy of branches whose flecked and slanted accents brush the river's surface, betrays a deeper source than sense: its shadow-play beguiles with its abstractions.

Maybe, ethereal in their artfulness, literally untouchable in style, shadows surrender us up to a world wherein the subtlety of what we feel marries the forms we see - in contemplation of whose transcendence only might we – fathered by imagination - be deathless and at last ideal.

14

Consummation

Imagine a landscape
Where everything meant something else:
A symbolic world full of significance you couldn't escape;

And you left standing there like a visionary Atlas
Effortlessly holding it up, as if the world were weightless;
Your conscience like a balloon in a breeze -

Or maybe you were Prometheus:
Set on fire by your gaze
Suddenly the dead sun, cold moon and remote stars amaze;

Oblivion redeemed in a blinding recall!
The whole of nature ablaze!
The sacred unity at last consuming all!

PENITENT

Hands clasped, head bowed:
What else should I confess
But the sin of rank dependence;

Of having recited a fool's catechism,
Of praying for my sick romanticism
To be healed by Nature's touch;

Of rifling the Romantic's medicine cabinet
For a panacea to cure
The degenerative disorder of my disillusionment;

Of resorting to the hackneyed consolation
Of cheap despair, rather than risk
The dark gold-mine lamp-lit by imagination;

Of suing to gods for states of grace,
Then blaspheming in a lonely temple,
When no divinity came to life in any marble face;

Of vandalising every niche, defacing each paragon,
Deaf to the iconoclastic sound within -
The broken was heart mine. The mind is its own pantheon.

I love the crows!
The recusant crows that never fly south;
That stand unannealed under unholy skies
And stare winter's hell in the mouth;
That endure and survive when everything dies.

I love the veteran crows
That ride out the warring wind's commands -
Bleak flock blown like a loose black cloak! -
That fight off the raptor when occasion demands;
That feast in the sun and hang on the oak!

I love the sinister crows
That fly in the face of sound reason;
Whose cowl-hooded covens utter a curse,
Invoking the dark, whatever the season;
That revel in death, and foretell the hearse;

I love the necromantic crows
That disport on the graves of the dead;
That pay no respect to their sleep,
But roister and frolic to wake them instead;
That dance where cadaverous worms creep.

Praise the crows! -
And all whose penance can never be done!
Praise the artistry that lives on its wits,
Hand-to-mouth in the sun;
That picks the bones clean and pulls clichés to bits!

Praise the crows!
And all who love, laugh and lament
At the grand theatre of fate; praise those
In the high farce of hell-fire heaven-sent!
Praise the carrion, black tragicomedy of crows!

BIRTHDAY OF THE UNCONQUERED SUN
('Dies natalis invicti solis' – Roman celebration day)

It has passed: the solstice in your frozen heart.
Now a kinder light intensifies:
New life gestates. Though winter played its part

In paring back delusion to the root; in nakedness
The tree of life stood threatened,
Its pulse against cold winds defenceless.

And so the sun returns just when all seems lost:
Like a sleeping princess kissed, the landscape wakes,
Love reaches out as sunlight melts the hardest frost.

Dusk asks for my identity: *I am the sky:*
The sunset is my descent into much deeper thought;
From its slow flares my beautiful dispassion wrought,
And in its amber clouds my doubts pass by.

CONSUMMATION

How consummate these late summer days,
When no new life struggles to be born,
And the sun extends a calm patrician gaze
Across the scion fields of stubbled corn.

How calm the quiet morning hours,
When migrant desire has flown,
And a native contentment strays
More near, for being left alone.

How languid the late afternoons,
The drowsy sense of ease,
The dreamy elegiac august moons
That haunt the twilit trees.

How unanxious the assembling clouds,
The harvest's success assured;
How soft the rain unfurled in shrouds
With no stormy omen untoward.

Now, at dusk, discharged of all desire,
Heart be happy, conscience still:
Let contentment tend a nightlong fire
To consume all doubt, ward away all ill.

These old, deserted stables mark a boundary:
The realm of loss and broken things.
Here, rust undoes all: in its inverse foundry,
I relish time's decaying furnishings;

Here, where defunct machinery prophesies
That whatever can be broken, shall be;
Here, where shattered glass reveals the lies
That hide the cracks in our fragility;

Where careless sunlight falls on broken tiles,
And purposelessness is the sole design;
As if time, itself, left to its own wiles,
Laid out an ironic mosaic of decline;

Here, in this eventless, empty coliseum,
Where no blood-red conflict lours;
Where only butterflies contest a lovely tedium
And poppies fleck the dusty hours;

Here, where silence builds a monastery
Around the holy relics of decay,
With no vain mention of self-mastery -
All tools of language stowed away;

Here, among things run to seed, gone bad,
The mind sifts its own derelictions,
And finds, with no incentive to be had,
Reality in ruins, peace without foundations....

OLD GODS IN A SHELTERED AREA

The cynic's ridicule contains a note of fear
At the unsophisticated truth it unearths here:
Love *is* a divine descent, a Spring, a Primavera.
Here, Aphrodite's advent melts my wintery soul,
Restoring sunlight, bringing warm days nearer.
In her shelter I'm returned to life, made whole;
The aegis of our intimacy is her fine weather:
In its courtyard, wine lies half drunk on the table,
Half in the Dionysian vessel of my heart. Together,
We enjoy a drunkenness that renders us more stable;
Mercury mysteriously animates the time we spend:
Keeping this temple-flame alive defines the friend,
Its stillness sacred: why move when thus enshrined?
Your love has always been a suntrap for my mind.

Modernity's an inferno: pagan art still pictures it best:
Trailing a mane of flame, our sun is riven
From night's rest. Careering at dawn's behest,
Across the sky, our love's chariot is driven.

Equine in spirit, bridled by time, reined in
By the world, handicapped by its forces,
We haul our load: chained in
Harmonious harness: Helios' golden horses

Burning westward tracks through blue space,
Friendship, the flaming curve we climb together,
Spurred on by each other's strength we race,
To breaking point test fate and fortune's tether!

Another day, another storm.
Merging with every squall of circumstance,
My mood's as tidal as the sea:
A strong current of contentment draws it on,
Regret is no longer the undertow
That drags me back into memory.

Such is the hydraulic action of the heart:
Something is eroding my old resistances:
Slowly I am changing shape:
Conscience is not a sandbar:
Ocean and river join: my life no longer silts up:
Nothing obstructs the longshore drift of the future.

As a drug addict I learned to disguise
The deep source of my distress;

Self-medicating a hit of nature's beauty to anaesthetise
My own subterranean ugliness.

But from now on I'll look myself in the eyes
And gratefully confess

That when I look out of my window
It's the view of me I see:

Nature has no meaning
Uncontributed by my humanity:

A rose doesn't know that it's red,
A mountain that it's majestic with distance;

While a poisonous berry gives a bird
The same delight a man takes in his bread.

We mete out judgements of beauty
In a scale that measures our needs:

Say, a sense of eternity in sunset,
Or of freedom in untrammelled seas.

Such are the calculations we make
To rule out the lie of our lands:-

The pain that we feel, or the pleasure we take
In hard words or a lover's soft hands:

The emotion I feel, the view that I see,
Depends on the place where I stand;

Likewise, returning my gaze through purblind eyes,
It's the view of me that awestruck Nature espies:

A creature whose mercurial mind affords
Him infinite form; who imagines paradise purely because he can:

This paragon of gods before whom nature bows:
This shape-shifting tragic evolutionary marvel, Man.

S et down this statute: the felony of fake self-reliance, confessed by a signature remorse, confers a penitential loneliness, with no prospect of review.

And yet, if I plead guilty to having forged a fraudulent identity, a false independence from my fellow men and women; subsequent experience also compels the admission of a virtue: *I have, at least, become an expert in imprisonment.*

As a diarist of solitary confinement, I am a meticulous chronicler of the forces that control my gaol. For a start, I know back-to-front how Nature governs a certain section of the prison: the hierarchy of command, what forces are at work *in her*, what drives her on, the musical pleasure she derives from my lyrical discomfiture - the fact that Nature sees me as a kind of entertainment, my hallucinations as a series of divertimenti - those times when, through want of company, through sheer sensory deprivation of any other soul, I would impotently rail against her and revile the natural phenomena of passing days, like a caged circus grotesque cursing passers-by; would excoriate sun, moon, stars and clouds for too little, or too much, heat, light, power; laud and lament the seasons' sensuality; fall in and out of love with sunsets, condemn the fickle beauty of the rose, or damn my own misplaced fidelity; - and then inevitably hear, in the dusty silence ensuing every outburst, the same sequence of mental cell doors slam shut in my mind, as Nature, warden-like, left dusk to descend and patrol my corridor....

And yet, recently, sometimes as evening falls, an unexpected equanimity has settled with the silence; sometimes, sitting here, assessing fate's prison patchwork design, I've begun to suspect the hand of strange necessity; have even entertained a dangerous proposition: *Could it be the punishment has worked?*

For, now, at last, it seems the term of my imprisonment is drawing to a final close. I have, both in writing and in person, applied for my release, and, realising I require no authority other than my own, have granted it myself today: the sentence served, the guilt discharged, the debt repaid.

So now all that's left is an ascent into the sunlight; yet not without a shade of apprehension, since the prospect of freedom greets ex-convicts with a set of doubts as strong as new restraints: day's avenues are long and wide, prison thoughts narrow and confined: *have I still sufficient constitution for contentment?* Or am I now dependent on long-fed habits of dejection? Have I, so long an inmate of self-imposed internment, become addicted to the narcotic consolations of the gaol - anaesthetised myself with easy drugs of resentment and regret?

And yet, if this were true, I would not be pushing past these prison bars, nor need to be restrained from running down the corridor, past the cells toward a tantalising open door.

Like a courier, my conscience has preceded me and performed the necessary paperwork: the trivial possessions to be reclaimed: jacket, shoes, watch, pen, some cash: - then out into the noonday sun: - shadowless courtyard of the hours: ante-room of liberty!

As for who, or what, awaits me on the other side: I'll greet the faces in the street with unerring, secret irony and tailored curiosity, in the private knowledge that each one, knowingly or unknowingly, has come to greet me.

Noonday sun: shadowless courtyard of the hours: ante-room of liberty!

One last time I stand beneath the squared-off prison sky, like a diver on a rock above a bay; stand upon the crest of day, surveying limitless sunlit sea. But first, one final look behind: that much every prisoner owes himself.

Gazing at the row of doors blatantly unpoliced, the open windows within reach, suddenly I see there never was a crime committed, nor punishment to endure - loneliness is an open gaol, a rehab-centre for voluntary inmates and somewhere along the line I forgot that I was just a visitor. For years, day's patient sunlit avenues have been waiting for me: - the cell door that I thought closed and locked forever –

had been left open all the time....

The Misanthropist's Secret Love-Life

www.ingramcontent.com/pod-product-compliance
Lightning Source LLC
Chambersburg PA
CBHW031318040426

42443CB00005B/131